INDIANA'S ROAD TO STATEHOOD

A DOCUMENTARY RECORD

Compiled by

HUBERT H. HAWKINS

INDIANA SESQUICENTENNIAL COMMISSION

Indianapolis, 1964

 16

INDIANA SESQUICENTENNIAL COMMISSION

(Members as of June, 1964)

EX-OFFICIO MEMBERS:

Matthew E. Welsh, *Governor*
Richard O. Ristine, *Lieutenant Governor*
Harold E. Achor, *Chief Justice of Supreme Court*
William E. Wilson, *Superintendent of Public Instruction*

APPOINTED MEMBERS:

Senator V. Dewey Annakin, Terre Haute
John V. Beamer, Wabash (Associate Chairman)*
I. George Blake, Franklin
Oliver C. Bumb, Muncie*
Donald F. Carmony, Bloomington (Chairman)*
Representative Leewell H. Carpenter, Wabash
Leo C. Craig, Delphi
Mrs. John R. Figg, Bloomington
Richard H. Gemmecke, Terre Haute*
John P. Goodwin, Brookville
Hubert H. Hawkins, Indianapolis*
Senator Bernard J. Krampe, Ferdinand
Mrs. William A. McKinzie, Indianapolis
Robert G. Moorhead, Indianapolis
Representative Paul B. Myers, Bloomingdale*
Edward D. Pierre, Indianapolis
Sister Maria Renata, Notre Dame
Charles Rochelle, Evansville
Hassil E. Schenck, Lebanon
Harry Smith, Connersville
Senator Lucius Somers, Hoagland
Representative George W. Stocksdale, Huntington
John Stover, Lafayette*
Mrs. Florence G. Watts, Vincennes
John Wilhelm, Hammond
Max Wright, Indianapolis

EXECUTIVE DIRECTOR:

Carl A. Zenor, 101 State Office Building

ADVISORY MEMBERS:

Milton B. Hale, Lieutenant Governor's Office
Robert McClarren, Director, Indiana State Library
Robert Starrett, Department of Conservation

---

* Member Executive Committee

ii

FOREWORD

In 1966 Hoosiers will observe the 150th anniversary of Indiana's admission to the United States. The Indiana General Assembly mandated the Indiana Sesquicentennial Commission to "prepare and execute plans for an historical and educational celebration of the sesquicentennial of the state." This booklet is one of the initial results of the work and planning of the Commission. It is designed principally for use in teaching Indiana history to junior high school students, but is quite suitable for all students of Indiana history.

This booklet fills a long-standing need and provides a collection of important documents suitable for students at the junior high school level as well as adult readers. These documents explain and illustrate how Indiana became the nineteenth member of the United States in 1816.

A careful study of this booklet can be very helpful in explaining and illustrating early American history as well as the beginnings of government in the Hoosier state. Early settlers of Indiana had considerable wisdom concerning politics and government. The documents here included—notably the 1816 Indiana State Constitution, Indiana's first—reflect such wisdom. Students and adults will find the booklet of great value and interest.

The Indiana Historical Bureau and McCormick Creek's State Park (Indiana's first state park) were the result of the observance of Indiana's centennial of statehood in 1916. It is hoped and expected that the observance of Indiana's 150th birthday as a member of the Union will result in increased interest in and support of the Indiana Historical Bureau, the Indiana State Library, and the Indiana state park system as well as for historical libraries, museums, and societies generally.

Every Hoosier has the responsibility for the continued support of these agencies of our state and our communities. Individual acceptance of this responsibility is essential if our history and our heritage are to be preserved and appreciated in a proper manner.

Hubert H. Hawkins has included in *Indiana's Road to Statehood: A Documentary Record* a very valuable collection of documents delineating Indiana's history. This booklet meets a timely need in an appropriate manner.

I congratulate all those who have worked so diligently on the project and the Indiana Sesquicentennial Celebration. Furthermore, I urge all Hoosiers to join in the observance of our 150th anniversary of statehood.

MATTHEW E. WELSH
Governor

State House
Indianapolis, 1964

PREFACE

As a contribution to the improved teaching of Indiana history, the Indiana Sesquicentennial Commission has authorized a series of booklets for classroom use. The first, a *Handbook on Indiana History,* by Donald F. Carmony, was published by the State Department of Public Instruction (1961) and re-issued by the Commission in 1963. This, the second booklet, consists of a selection of documents relating to the transition from territory to statehood.

As Charles Langlois put it, "The historian works with documents. Documents are the traces which have been left by the thoughts and actions of men of former time." This dictum has a double implication: First, the documents of Indiana history—the letters, public records, diaries, memoirs, business records, etc.—must be preserved for the researcher's use. Second, selected documents can be extremely useful in the teaching of history. The thoughtful reading of an important original document will always be a more exciting and significant educational experience than the perusing of a secondary account.

While most of the documents included in *Indiana's Road to Statehood* may be found in a number of publications, many of them are not easily accessible in convenient form for classroom use. The text used has been that of the source first cited in the multiple footnotes. Introductory comment has been restricted, partly because of space considerations, but also in the belief that the teacher will use the documents more effectively after making an independent analysis. The undersigned readily concedes that another compiler might have chosen a somewhat different, and perhaps better, list of documents, however he believes a majority of the items selected would appear on any such list.

The compiler wishes to thank Dr. Donald F. Carmony, Chairman of the Indiana Sesquicentennial Commission, and Mr. Carl Zenor, the Commission's Executive Director, for valuable assistance, but he claims exclusive responsibility for errors and other shortcomings. Teachers of Indiana history have done an amazingly good job despite inadequacies of preparation and materials. It is earnestly hoped that this booklet may be useful in the more effective teaching of this important subject.

Hubert H. Hawkins
Director, Indiana Historical Bureau
Secretary, Indiana Historical Society
Indianapolis, 1964

CONTENTS

INDIANA'S ROAD TO STATEHOOD:
A DOCUMENTARY RECORD

On December 11, 1816, President James Madison approved the "Resolution for admitting the State of Indiana into the Union."[1] Indiana was thus the nineteenth state to join the Union and the second to be created from the Old Northwest. Indiana was born of the westward movement. As one observer noted, "Old America seems to be breaking up and moving westward."[2] The pioneers who settled Indiana came from the seaboard and the older settlements west of the Alleghenies. A few came from New England, more from the middle states, but the majority were from the Carolinas and Virginia, either directly, or by way of Tennessee, Kentucky, and Ohio.

These early settlers sought a freer and richer life for themselves and their children. They wanted to cut fertile farms from the Indiana forest. They wanted to live in a more democratic society than then existed in "Old America." They wanted to enjoy the many opportunities, economic, political, and social, that could only be found in the new West. Some wanted to escape the blighting influence of slavery. Self-government was in their blood. It was "what the American Revolution had been about." The early Hoosiers tolerated the restrictions of territorial government with scant patience and yearned for the greater liberty they expected statehood to bring.

The evolvement and acceptance of a policy whereby new and sparsely populated areas might aspire to membership in the Union "on an equal footing with the original States, in all respects whatever"[3] was both wise and enlightened. It was basic to the integrity and growth of the American Republic. A discredited colonialism was the alternative. The adoption of this policy in the Congress of the Confederation and in the United States Constitution was of major significance. As the Indiana Sesquicentennial nears (1966) it seems appropriate and useful to review the essential steps toward Indiana statehood. The pattern, with some variation, became standard in an expanding Union.

The French were the first Europeans to control the land that was to become Indiana. LaSalle crossed the northwestern corner of the state in 1679. The French built an extensive but ephemeral colonial empire based upon the St. Lawrence and Mississippi Valleys which lasted until 1763. This vast territory was divided into two provinces, Louisiana and Canada, thinly held by a sparse population of habitants, priests, soldiers and traders.

---

[1] *Annals of the Congress of the United States,* 14 Cong., 2 Sess., 1348.
[2] Morris Birkbeck, *Notes on a Journey in America, from the Coast of Virginia to the Territory of Illinois* . . . (3d ed., London, 1818), 31.
[3] *Annals of Congress,* 14 Cong., 2 Sess., 1348.

1

Three centers of French influence were established in Indiana: Post Miami where Fort Wayne now stands, Ouiatanon near the present city of Lafayette and Vincennes on the lower Wabash. Vincennes was administered from New Orleans and was a part of Louisiana; Post Miami and Ouiatanon were in Canada and responsible to Quebec. The main line of communication between the two provinces followed the Wabash River across Indiana.

Since the earliest days of English settlement England had also claimed the hinterland of which Indiana was a part. Virginia had pretensions to the Ohio Country under its charter of 1609. Three conflicts between England and France resulted from dynastic clashes in Europe between 1689 and 1748. Each had its American aspect. A fourth, the French and Indian War, started in America in 1754 over the control of the upper Ohio Valley and its rich fur trade. After nine years of fighting the French were beaten and the English had to decide what to demand of their humbled rival.

British leaders were not agreed upon the matter of spoils. Were not the rich sugar islands of the West Indies more valuable than the trackless forests of continental America? Would the removal of French power from America lessen the loyal dependence of the British Americans upon Great Britain? William Pitt, when prime minister, summed it up when he asked the House of Commons: "Some are for keeping Canada; some, Guadaloupe; who will tell me which I shall be hanged for not keeping?"[4] This decision vitally concerned the future of the Ohio Country and what was to be Indiana. After a bitter controversy, the British elected to take France's continental holdings. In the Treaty of Paris (1763) France yielded all of her territory east of the Mississippi, except a small area around New Orleans, to Britain.

Peace brought monumental problems to the expanded British Empire. In an effort to appease the restless Indians, the Proclamation of 1763 was issued which forbade American settlement west of the Alleghenies. The unpopular Quebec Act (1774) attached the Ohio Country to Quebec for purposes of government. Both contributed to the growing tension between the American colonists and the imperial government which was to culminate in the American Revolution.

Despite the King's proclamation, the westward movement continued. At the time of the Revolution a handful of settlers held Kentucky for Virginia. The Kentucky posts sustained a savage assault by British-supplied Indian raiders from northwest of the Ohio. George Rogers Clark, a dynamic young frontiersman with a talent for leadership, persuaded Governor Patrick Henry of Virginia that the Northwest must be conquered if Kentucky were to survive. Acting under the authority of Vir-

---

4 G. F. Russell Barker (ed.), *Horace Walpole: Memoirs of the Reign of King George the Third* (4 vols., London, 1894), I, 26; for a detailed account of this controversy, see Clarence W. Alvord, *The Mississippi Valley in British Politics* . . . (2nd ed., 2 vols., New York, 1959), I, 19-76.

ginia, Clark seized the Illinois towns and extended his control to Vincennes in 1778. When, in the late fall, the British position at Vincennes was re-established by Lieutenant Governor Henry Hamilton, Clark led a force of 172 men in a heroic mid-winter march through flooded country from Kaskaskia to Vincennes. After a short siege Hamilton was forced to surrender, February 25, 1779.

Clark's operations northwest of the Ohio may have had some influence on the cession of this area to the Americans in the treaty that followed the Revolution (1783). Without doubt it strengthened Virginia's title.[5] Upon learning of Clark's successes the Virginia legislature adopted a law organizing all the territory northwest of the Ohio as the County of Illinois. Governor Henry appointed Colonel John Todd as county lieutenant. After his arrival in May, 1779, Todd arranged for civil elections in the several settlements but accomplished little more. The county lieutenant was certainly lacking in public resources and probably in personal ones. He eventually went to Kentucky and failed to return.[6]

Possibly Virginia's neglect of the County of Illinois grew out of a realization that it would not be feasible to keep it. Those states lacking substantial claims to western lands vigorously opposed the pretensions of states like Virginia. Maryland became a spokesman for the have-not states. The Maryland delegates presented the "instructions of the general assembly of Maryland" on the subject to Congress on May 21, 1779. Maryland asked:

> Is it possible that those states, who are ambitiously grasping at territories, to which in our judgment they have not the least shadow of exclusive right, will use with greater moderation the increase of wealth and power derived from those territories, when acquired, than what they have displayed in their endeavours to acquire them? we think not; we are convinced the same spirit which hath prompted them to insist on a claim so extravagant . . . so incompatible with the general welfare of all the states, will urge them on to add oppression to injustice.

The Marylanders argued that Virginia might "draw into her treasury vast sums of money" from the sales of western lands, reduce her taxes, and drain the population and wealth from neighboring states not so endowed.[7]

New York, whose title to western territory was somewhat tenuous, offered to yield it in February, 1780, and did so the next year. In

---

[5] Samuel F. Bemis, *The Diplomacy of the American Revolution* (New York, 1935), 219 n.; J. A. James, *Oliver Pollock* (New York, 1937), 242-248.
[6] Jacob P. Dunn, *Indiana and Indianans* . . . (5 vols., Chicago, 1919), I, 169-170, 180-181. Clarence W. Alvord (ed.), *Cahokia Records, 1778-1790 (Collections of the Illinois State Historical Library*, vol. II, Springfield, 1907), 9-11; "Col. John Todd's Record-Book," in *Illinois in the Eighteenth Century*, by Edward G. Mason, *(Fergus Historical Series*, No. 12, Chicago, 1881), 49-68.
[7] Worthington C. Ford *et al.* (eds.), *Journals of the Continental Congress, 1774-1789* (34 vols., Washington, 1910), XIV, 619-22.

September, 1780, Congress decided "to press upon those states which can remove the embarrassment respecting the western country, a liberal surrender of a portion of their territorial claims, since they cannot be preserved entire without endangering the stability of the general confederacy."[8] On October 10, Congress resolved:

That the unappropriated lands that may be ceded or relinquished to the United States, by any particular states, pursuant to the recommendation of Congress of the 6 day of September last, shall be . . . disposed of for the common benefit of . . . the United States . . . and be settled and formed into distinct republican states, which shall become members of the federal union, and have the same rights of sovereignty, freedom and independence, as the other states. . . .[9]

[8] *Ibid.*, XVII, 806-07.
[9] *Ibid.*, XVIII, 915.

THE VIRGINIA CESSION

On January 2, 1781, Virginia offered to cede her northwestern lands but attached conditions unacceptable to Congress. On December 20, 1783, the Virginia legislature modified its position and passed the Virginia Act of Cession. The other states with western claims subsequently relinquished them, in several instances stipulating reserves. The Virginia Deed of Cession was formally delivered to and accepted by Congress on March 1, 1784:[10]

(March 1, 1784)

To all who shall see these presents, we Thomas Jefferson, Samuel Hardy, Arthur Lee and James Monroe the underwritten delegates for the Commonwealth in Virginia, in the Congress of the United States of America, send Greeting:

Whereas the general assembly of the Commonwealth of Virginia at their sessions begun on the 20th day of October, 1783, passed an act, entitled "An Act to authorize the delegates of this State in Congress to convey to the United States in Congress assembled, all the right of this commonwealth, to the territory northwestward of the river Ohio." in these words following to wit:

"Whereas the Congress of the United States did, by their act of the sixth day of September in the year 1780, recommend to the several states in the Union, having claims to waste and unappropriated lands in the western country, a liberal cession to the United States, of a portion of their respective claims for the common benefit of the Union: and whereas this Commonwealth did, on the 2d day of January, in the year 1781, yield to the Congress of the United States, for the benefit of the said states, all right, title and claim which the said Commonwealth had to the territory northwest of the river Ohio, subject to the conditions annexed to the said act of cession. And whereas the United States in Congress assembled, have, by their act of the 13th of September last, stipulated the terms on which they agree to accept the cession of this State, should the legislature approve thereof, which terms, although they do not come fully up to the propositions of this Commonwealth, are conceived on the whole, to

[10] *Ibid.*, XXVI, 113-117; Charles Kettleborough (ed.), *Constitution Making in Indiana* . . . (2 vols., Indianapolis, 1916), I, 9-15; Clarence E. Carter (ed.), *The Territorial Papers of the United States* (vols. I-, Washington, 1934-), II, 6-9.

approach so nearly to them, as to induce this State to accept thereof, in full confidence, that Congress will in justice to this State, for the liberal cession she hath made, earnestly press upon the other states claiming large tracts of waste and uncultivated territory, the propriety of making cessions equally liberal, for the common benefit and support of the union. Be it enacted by the General Assembly, that it shall and may be lawful for the delegates of this State, to the Congress of the United States, or such of them as shall be assembled in Congress, and the said delegates, or such of them so assembled, are hereby fully authorized and empowered, for and on behalf of this State, by proper deeds or instrument in writing, under their hands and seals, to convey, transfer, assign and make over unto the United States in Congress assembled, for the benefit of the said states, all right, title and claim, as well of soil as jurisdiction, which this Commonwealth hath to the territory or tract of country within the limits of the Virginia charter, situate, lying and being to the northwest of the river Ohio, subject to the terms and conditions contained in the before recited act of Congress, of the 13th day of September last; that is to say, upon condition that the territory so ceded, shall be laid out and formed into states, containing a suitable extent of territory, not less than one hundred, nor more than one hundred and fifty miles square, or as near thereto as circumstances will admit; and that the states so formed, shall be distinct republican states, and admitted members of the federal union; having the same rights of sovereignty, freedom and independence, as the other states. That the necessary and reasonable expences incurred by this State, in subduing any British posts, or in maintaining forts or garrisons within, and for the defence, or in acquiring any part of the territory so ceded or relinquished, shall be fully reimbursed by the United States: and that one commissioner shall be appointed by Congress, one by this Commonwealth, and another by those two commissioners, who, or a majority of them, shall be authorized and empowered to adjust and liquidate the account of the necessary and reasonable expences incurred by this State, which they shall judge to be comprised within the intent and meaning of the act of Congress, of the 10th of October, 1780, respecting such expences. That the French and Canadian inhabitants, and other settlers of the Kaskaskies, St. Vincents, and the neighboring villages who have professed themselves citizens of Virginia, shall have their possessions and titles confirmed to them, and be protected in the enjoyment of their rights and liberties. That a quantity not exceeding one hundred and fifty thousand acres of land, promised by this State, shall be allowed and granted to the then Colonel, now General George Rogers Clarke, and to the officers and soldiers of his regiment, who marched with him when the posts of Kaskaskies and St. Vincents were reduced, and to the officers and soldiers that have been since incorporated into the said regiment, to be laid off in one tract, the length of which not to exceed double the breadth, in such place on the northwest side of the Ohio, as a majority of the officers shall choose, and to be after-wards divided among the said officers and soldiers in due proportion, according to the laws of Virginia. That in case the quantity of good lands on the southeast side of the Ohio, upon the waters of Cumberland river, and between the Green river and Tennessee river, which have been reserved by law for the Virginia Troops upon continental estab-lishment, should, from the North Carolina line, bearing in further upon the Cumberland lands than was expected, prove insufficient for their legal bounties, the deficiency should be made up to the said troops, in good lands, to be laid off between the rivers Scioto, and Little Miami, on the northwest side of the river Ohio, in such propor-tions as have been engaged to them by the laws of Virginia. That all the lands within the territory so ceded to the United States, and not reserved for or appropriated to any of the before-mentioned purposes, or disposed of in bounties to the officers and soldiers of the American army, shall be considered as a common fund for the use and benefit of such of the United States, as have become or shall become members of the confederation or federal alliance of the said states, Virginia inclusive, according to their usual respective proportions in the general charge and expenditure, and shall be faithfully and *bona fide* disposed of for that purpose, and for no other use or purpose whatsoever. Provided that the trust hereby reposed in the delegates of this State, shall not be executed, unless three of them at least are present in Congress."

And whereas the said general assembly, by their resolution of June 6th, 1783, had constituted and appointed us the said Thomas Jefferson, Samuel Hardy, Arthur Lee, and James Monroe, delegates to represent the said Commonwealth in Congress for one year, from the first Monday in November then next following, which resolution remains in full force: Now therefore know ye that we the said Thomas Jefferson, Samuel Hardy, Arthur Lee, and James Monroe, by virtue of the power and authority committed to us by the act of the said general assembly of Virginia before recited, and in the name, and for and on behalf of the said Commonwealth, do by these presents convey, transfer, assign, and make over unto the United States in Congress Assembled, for the benefit of the said states, Virginia inclusive, all right, title and claim, as well of soil as of jurisdiction, which the said Commonwealth hath to the territory or tract of country within the limits of the Virginia charter, situate, lying and being to the northwest of the river Ohio, to and for the uses and purposes, and on the conditions of the said recited act. In testimony whereof, we have hereunto subscribed our names and affixed our seals, in Congress, the [first] day of [March] in the year of our Lord one thousand and seven hundred and eighty-four, and of the independence of the United States the eighth."

LAND ORDINANCE OF 1785

With the cession of the state lands assured, Congress proceeded to administer the new national domain. An ordinance was adopted on May 20, 1785, which laid the foundations of American land policy until the passage of the Homestead Act in 1862. After the Indian title had been purchased the ceded lands were to be systematically surveyed, prior to sale or settlement, into townships six miles square. Of the thirty-six sections of 640 acres in each township, the sixteenth was reserved "for the maintenance of public schools." After the survey the land might be offered for sale at public auction in units of a section or more at a minimum price of $1.00 per acre. Few settlers had the necessary capital to make so large a purchase and the debt-ridden national government received a relatively small revenue from its lands until the terms of sale were liberalized.[11]

An Ordinance for ascertaining the mode of disposing of Lands in the Western Territory.

Be it ordained by the United States in Congress assembled, that the territory ceded by individual States to the United States, which has been purchased of the Indian inhabitants, shall be disposed of in the following manner:

A surveyor from each state shall be appointed by Congress, or a committee of the States, who shall take an Oath for the faithful discharge of his duty, before the Geographer of the United States, who is hereby empowered and directed to administer the same; and the like oath shall be administered to each chain carrier, by the surveyor under whom he acts.

The Geographer, under whose direction the surveyors shall act, shall occasionally form such regulations for their conduct, as he shall deem necessary; and shall have authority to suspend them for misconduct in Office, and shall make report of the same to Congress or to the Committee of the States; and he shall make report in case of sickness, death, or resignation of any surveyor.

The Surveyors, as they are respectively qualified, shall proceed to divide the said territory into townships of six miles square, by

---

11 *Journals of the Continental Congress,* XXVIII, 375-81; Carter(ed.), *Territorial Papers,* II, 12-18; Henry S. Commager (ed.), *Documents of American History* (6th ed., New York, 1958), 123-24; also see John D. Barnhart and Donald F. Carmony, *Indiana: From Frontier to Industrial Commonwealth* (4 vols., New York, 1954), I, 75-76; or Roy M. Robbins, *Our Landed Heritage: The Public Domain, 1776-1936* (Princeton, 1942), 3-19.

lines running due north and south, and others crossing these at right angles, as near as may be, unless where the boundaries of the late Indian purchases may render the same impracticable, and then they shall depart from this rule no farther than such particular circumstances may require; and each surveyor shall be allowed and paid at the rate of two dollars for every mile, in length, he shall run, including the wages of chain carriers, markers, and every other expense attending the same.

The first line, running north and south as aforesaid, shall begin on the river Ohio, at a point that shall be found to be due north from the western termination of a line, which has been run as the southern boundary of the state of Pennsylvania; and the first line, running east and west, shall begin at the same point, and shall extend throughout the whole territory. Provided, that nothing herein shall be construed, as fixing the western boundary of the state of Pennsylvania. The geographer shall designate the townships, or fractional parts of townships, by numbers progressively from south to north; always beginning each range with number one; and the ranges shall be distinguished by their progressive numbers to the westward. The first range, extending from the Ohio to the lake Erie, being marked number one. The geographer shall personally attend to the running of the first east and west line; and shall take the latitude of the extremes of the first north and south line, and of the mouths of the principal rivers.

The lines shall be measured with a chain; shall be plainly marked by chaps on the trees and exactly described on a plat; whereon shall be noted by the surveyor, at their proper distances, all mines, salt springs, salt licks and mill seats, that shall come to his knowledge, and all water courses, mountains and other remarkable and permanent things, over and near which such lines shall pass, and also the quality of the lands.

The plats of the townships respectively, shall be marked by subdivisions into lots of one mile square, or 640 acres, in the same direction as the external lines, and numbered from 1 to 36; always beginning the succeeding range of the lots with the number next to that with which the preceding one concluded. And where, from the causes before mentioned, only a fractional part of a township shall be surveyed, the lots protracted thereon, shall bear the same numbers as if the township had been entire. And the surveyors, in running the external lines of the townships, shall, at the interval of every mile, mark corners for the lots which are adjacent, always designating the same in a different manner from those of the townships.

The geographer and surveyors shall pay the utmost attention to the variation of the magnetic needle; and shall run and note all lines by the true meridian, certifying, with every plat, what was the variation at the times of running the lines thereon noted.

As soon as seven ranges of townships, and fractional parts of townships, in the direction from south to north, shall have been surveyed, the geographer shall transmit plats thereof to the board of treasury, who shall record the same with the report, in well bound books to be kept for that purpose. And the geographer shall make similar returns, from time to time, of every seven ranges as they may be surveyed. The Secretary at War shall have recourse thereto, and shall take by lot therefrom, a number of townships, and fractional parts of townships, as well from those to be sold entire as from those to be sold in lots, as will be equal to one seventh part of the whole of such seven ranges, as nearly as may be, for the use of the late continental army; and he shall make a similar draught, from time to time, until a sufficient quantity is drawn to satisfy the same, to be applied in manner hereinafter directed. The board of treasury shall, from time to time, cause the remaining numbers, as well those to be sold entire, as those to be sold in lots, to be drawn for, in the name of the thirteen states respectively, according to the quotas in the last preceding requisition on all the states; provided, that in case more land than its proportion is allotted for sale, in any state, at any distribution, a deduction be made therefor at the next.

The board of treasury shall transmit a copy of the original plats, previously noting thereon, the townships, and fractional parts of townships, which shall have fallen to the several states, by the distribution aforesaid, to the Commissioners of the loan office of the several states, who, after giving notice of not less than two nor more than six months by causing advertisements to be posted up at the court houses, or other noted places in every county, and to be inserted in one newspaper, published in the states of their residence respectively, shall proceed to sell the townships, or fractional parts of townships, at public vendue, in the following manner, viz.: The township, or fractional part of a township, N 1, in the first range, shall be sold entire; and N 2, in the same range, by lots; and thus in alternate order through the whole of the first range. The township, or fractional part of a township, N 1, in the second range, shall be sold by lots; and N 2, in the same range, entire; and so in alternate order through the whole of the second range; and the third range shall be sold in the same manner as the first, and the fourth in the same manner as the second, and thus alternately throughout all the ranges; provided, that none of the lands, within the said territory, be sold under the price of one dollar the acre, to be paid in specie, or loan office certificates, reduced to specie value, by the scale of depreciation, or certificates of liquidated debts of the United States, including interest, besides the expense of the survey and other charges thereon, which are hereby rated at thirty six dollars the township, in specie or certificates as aforesaid, and so in the same proportion for a fractional part of a township, or of a lot, to be paid at the time of sales; on failure of which payment the said lands shall again be offered for sale.

There shall be reserved for the United States out of every township, the four lots, being numbered 8, 11, 26, 29, and out of every fractional part of a township, so many lots of the same numbers as shall be found thereon, for future sale. There shall be reserved the lot N 16, of every township, for the maintenance of public schools, within the said township; also one third part of all gold, silver, lead and copper mines, to be sold, or otherwise disposed of as Congress shall hereafter direct.

When any township, or fractional part of a township, shall have been sold as aforesaid, and the money or certificates received therefor, the loan officer shall deliver a deed in the following terms:

The United States of America to all to whom these presents shall come, greeting:

Know ye, That for the consideration of [blank] dollars we have granted, and hereby do grant and confirm unto [blank] the township, (or fractional part of a township, as the case may be) numbered [blank] in the range [blank] excepting therefrom, and reserving one third part of all gold, silver, lead and copper mines within the same; and the lots Ns 8, 11, 26, and 29, for future sale or disposition, and the lot N 16, for the maintenance of public schools. To have to the said [blank] his heirs and assigns for ever; (or if more than one purchaser to the said [blank] their heirs and assigns for ever as tenants in Common.) In witness whereof, (A.B.) Commissioner of the loan office, in the State of [blank] hath, in conformity to the Ordinance passed by the United States in Congress assembled, the twentieth day of May, in the year of our Lord one thousand seven hundred and eighty five, hereunto set his hand and affixed his seal this [blank] day of [blank] in the year of our Lord [blank] and of the independence of the United States of America [blank].

And when any township, or fractional part of a township, shall be sold by lots as aforesaid, the Commissioner of the loan office shall deliver a deed therefor in the following form:

The United States of America to all to whom these presents shall come, Greeting:

Know ye, That for the consideration of [blank] dollars, we have granted, and hereby do grant and confirm unto [blank] the lot (or lots, as the case may be, in the township or fractional part of the township, as the case may be) numbered [blank] in the range [blank] excepting and reserving one third part of all gold, silver, lead and copper mines within the same, for future sale or disposition. To have to the said [blank] his heirs and assigns for ever; (or if more than one purchaser, to the said [blank] their heirs and assigns for ever as tenants in common.) In witness whereof, (A.B.) Commissioner of the continental loan office in the state of [blank] hath, in conformity to the Ordinance passed by the United States in Congress assembled, the twentieth day of May, in the year of our Lord 1785, hereunto set his hand and affixed his seal, this [blank] day of [blank] in the year of our Lord [blank] and of the independence of the United States of America [blank].

Which deeds shall be recorded in proper books by the commissioner of the loan office and shall be certified to have been recorded, previous to their being delivered to the purchaser, and shall be good and valid to convey the lands in the same described.

The commissioners of the loan offices respectively, shall transmit to the board of treasury every three months, an account of the townships, fractional parts of townships, and lots committed to their charge; specifying therein the names of the persons to whom sold, and the sums of money or certificates received for the same; and shall cause all certificates by them received, to be struck through with a circular punch; and they shall be duly charged in the books of the treasury, with the amount of the moneys or certificates, distinguishing the same, by them received as aforesaid.

If any township, or fractional part of a township or lot, remains unsold for eighteen months after the plat shall have been received, by the commissioners of the loan office, the same shall be returned to the board of treasury, and shall be sold in such manner as Congress may hereafter direct

And whereas Congress by their resolutions of September 16 and 18 in the year 1776, and the 12th of August, 1780, stipulated grants of land to certain officers and soldiers of the late continental army, and by the resolution of the 22d September, 1780, stipulated grants of land to certain officers in the hospital department of the late continental army; for complying therefore with such engagements, Be it ordained, That the secretary at war, from the returns in his office, or such other evidence as the nature of the case may admit, determine who are the objects of the above resolutions and engagements, and the quantity of land to which such persons or their representatives are respectively entitled, and cause the townships, or fractional parts of townships, hereinbefore reserved for the use of the late continental army, to be drawn for in such manner as he shall deem expedient, to answer the purpose of an impartial distribution. He shall, from time to time, transmit certificates to the commissioners of the loan offices of the different states, to the lines of which the military claimants have respectively belonged, specifying the name and rank of the party, the terms of his engagement and time of his service, and the division, brigade, regiment or company to which he belonged, the quantity of land he is entitled to, and the township, or fractional part of a township, and range out of which his portion is to be taken.

The commissioners of the loan offices shall execute deeds for such undivided proportions in manner and form herein before-mentioned, varying only in such a degree as to make the same conformable to the certificate from the Secretary at War.

Where any military claimants of bounty in lands shall not have belonged to the line of any particular state, similar certificates shall be sent to the board of treasury, who shall execute deeds to the parties for the same.

The Secretary at War, from the proper returns, shall transmit to the board of treasury, a certificate specifying the name and rank of the several claimants of the hospital department of the late continental army, together with the quantity of land each claimant is entitled to, and the township, or fractional part of a township, and range out of which his portion is to be taken; and thereupon the board of treasury shall proceed to execute deeds to such claimants.

The board of treasury, and the commissioners of the loan offices in the states, shall, within 18 months, return receipts to the secretary at war, for all deeds which have been delivered, as also all the original deeds which remain in their hands for want of applicants, having been first recorded; which deeds so returned, shall be preserved in the office, until the parties or their representatives require the same.

And be it further Ordained, That three townships adjacent to lake Erie be reserved, to be hereafter disposed of by Congress, for the use of the officers, men and others, refugees from Canada, and the refugees from Nova Scotia, who are or may be entitled to grants of land under resolutions of Congress now existing, or which may hereafter be made respecting them, and for such other purposes as Congress may hereafter direct.

And be it further Ordained, That the towns of Gnadenhutten, Schoenbrun and Salem, on the Muskingum, and so much of the lands adjoining to the said towns, with the buildings and improvements thereon, shall be reserved for the sole use of the Christian Indians, who were formerly settled there, or the remains of that society, as may, in the judgment of the geographer, be sufficient for them to cultivate.

Saving and reserving always, to all officers and soldiers entitled to lands on the northwest side of the Ohio, by donation or bounty from the commonwealth of Virginia, and to all persons claiming under them, all rights to which they are so entitled, under the deed of cession executed by the delegates for the state of Virginia, on the first day of March, 1784, and the act of Congress accepting the same: and to the end that the said rights may be fully and effectually secured, according to the true intent and meaning of the said deed of cession and act aforesaid, Be it Ordained, that no part of the land included between the rivers called little Miami and Sciota, on the northwest side of the river Ohio, be sold, or in any manner alienated, until there shall first have been laid off and appropriated for the said Officers and Soldiers, and persons claiming under them, the lands they are entitled to, agreeably to the said deed of cession and act of Congress accepting the same.

Done by the United States in Congress assembled, the 20th day of May, in the year of our Lord 1785, and of our sovereignty and independence the ninth.

Charles Thomson, *Secretary*.　　　　　　　　Richard H. Lee, *President*.

THE NORTHWEST ORDINANCE, 1787

A committee had submitted a report to Congress on the government of the western territory on April 23, 1784. It was largely based on a plan proposed by Thomas Jefferson although the anti-slavery provision he advocated was defeated by a vote of seven states to six. The interest of the Ohio Company in colonizing the Ohio Country led Congress to enact a definitive plan of government on July 13, 1787. In the initial stage the Northwest Ordinance provided for a highly centralized government with no popular participation. A legislature, elected with property qualifications, was authorized when the Territory's male population numbered five thousand adults. The governor was given an absolute veto. But the ordinance included a prohibition against slavery, provision for a democratic system of inheritance, and a bill of rights. No less than three nor more than five state should be formed from the territory. A minimum population of sixty thousand was required for statehood:[12]

An Ordinance for the government of the territory of the United States North West of the river Ohio.

Be it ordained by the United States in Congress Assembled that the said territory for the purposes of temporary government be one district, subject however to be divided into two districts as future circumstances may in the Opinion of Congress make it expedient.

Be it ordained by the authority aforesaid, that the estates both of resident and non-resident proprietors in the said territory dying intestate shall descend to and be distributed among their children and the descendants of a deceased child in equal parts; the descendants of a deceased child or grandchild to take the share of their deceased parent in equal parts among them; and where there shall be no children or descendants then in equal parts to the next of kin in equal degree and among collaterals the children of a deceased brother or sister of the intestate shall have in equal parts among them their deceased parent's share and there shall in no case be a distinction between kindred of the whole and half blood; saving in all cases to the widow of the intestate her third part of the real estate for life, and one third part of the personal estate; and this law relative to descents and dower shall remain in full force until altered by the legislature of the district. And

---

[12] *Journals of the Continental Congress,* XXXII, 334-343; Carter (ed.), *Territorial Papers,* II, 39-50; Kettleborough (ed.), *Constitution Making in Indiana,* I, 26-33; Barnhart and Carmony, *Indiana,* I, 82-83; Beverley W. Bond, Jr., *The Civilization of the Old Northwest* . . . (New York, 1934), 9-10.

until the governor and judges shall adopt laws as herein after mentioned estates in the said territory may be devised or bequeathed by wills in writing signed and sealed by him or her in whom the estate may be, being of full age and attested by three witnesses, and real estates may be conveyed by lease and release or bargain and sale signed, sealed and delivered by the person being of full age in whom the estate may be and attested by two witnesses provided such wills be duly proved and such conveyances be acknowledged or the execution thereof duly proved and be recorded within one year after proper magistrates, courts and registers shall be appointed for that purpose and personal property may be transferred by delivery saving however to the french and canadian inhabitants and other settlers of the Kaskaskies, Saint Vincents and neighbouring villages who have heretofore professed themselves citizens of Virginia, their laws and customs now in force among them relative to the descent and conveyance of property.

Be it ordained by the authority aforesaid that there shall be appointed from time to time by Congress a governor, whose commission shall continue in force for the term of three years, unless sooner revoked by Congress; he shall reside in the district and have a freehold estate therein, in one thousand acres of land while in the exercise of his office. There shall be appointed from time to time by Congress a secretary, whose commission shall continue in force for four years, unless sooner revoked; he shall reside in the district and have a freehold estate therein in five hundred acres of land while in the exercise of his office; It shall be his duty to keep and preserve the acts and laws passed by the legislature and the public records of the district and the proceedings of the governor in his executive department and transmit authentic copies of such acts and proceedings every six months to the Secretary of Congress. There shall also be appointed a court to consist of three judges any two of whom to form a court, who shall have a common law jurisdiction and reside in the district and have each therein a freehold estate in five hundred acres of land while in the exercise of their offices, and their commissions shall continue in force during good behaviour.

The governor, and judges or a majority of them shall adopt and publish in the district such laws of the original states criminal and civil as may be necessary and best suited to the circumstances of the district and report them to Congress from time to time, which laws shall be in force in the district until the organization of the general assembly therein, unless disapproved of by Congress; but afterwards the legislature shall have authority to alter them as they shall think fit.

The governor for the time being shall be Commander in Chief of the militia, appoint and commission all officers in the same below the rank of general Officers; All general Officers shall be appointed and commissioned by Congress.

Previous to the Organization of the general Assembly the governor shall appoint such magistrates and other civil officers in each county or township, as he shall find necessary for the preservation of the peace and good order in the same. After the general Assembly shall be organized, the powers and duties of magistrates and other civil officers shall be regulated and defined by the said Assembly; but all magistrates and other civil officers, not herein otherwise directed shall during the continuance of this temporary government be appointed by the governor.

For the prevention of crimes and injuries the laws to be adopted or made shall have force in all parts of the district and for the execution of process criminal and civil, the governor shall make proper divisions thereof, and he shall proceed from time to time as circumstances may require to lay out the parts of the district in which the indian titles shall have been extinguished into counties and townships subject however to such alterations as may thereafter be made by the legislature.

So soon as there shall be five thousand free male inhabitants of full age in the district upon giving proof thereof to the governor, they shall receive authority with time and place to elect representatives from their counties or townships to represent them in the general assembly, provided that for every five hundred free male inhabitants there shall be one representative and so on progressively with the number of free male inhabitants shall the right of representation encrease until the number of representatives shall amount to twenty five after which the number and proportion of representatives shall be regulated by the legislature; provided that no person be eligible or qualified to act as a representative unless he shall have been a citizen of one of the United States three years and be a resident in the district or unless he shall have resided in the district three years and in either case shall likewise hold in his own right in fee simple two hundred acres of land within the same; provided also that a freehold in fifty acres of land in the district having been a citizen of one of the states and being resident in the district; or the like freehold and two years residence in the district shall be necessary to qualify a man as an elector of a representative.

The representatives thus elected shall serve for the term of two years and in case of the death of a representative or removal from office, the governor shall issue a writ to the county or township for which he was a member, to elect another in his stead to serve for the residue of the term.

The general assembly or legislature shall consist of the governor, legislative council and a house of representatives. The legislative council shall consist of five members to continue in Office five years unless sooner removed by Congress any three of whom to be a quorum and the members of the council shall be nominated and appointed in the following manner, to wit: As soon as representatives shall be elected, the governor shall appoint a time and place for them to meet together, and when met they shall nominate ten persons residents in the district and each possessed of a freehold in five hundred acres of Land and return their names to Congress; five of whom Congress shall appoint and commission to serve as aforesaid; and whenever a vacancy shall happen in the council by death or removal from office, the house of representatives shall nominate two persons qualified as aforesaid, for each vacancy, and return their names to Congress, one of whom Congress shall appoint and commission for the residue of the term, and every five years, four months at least before the expiration of the time of service of the Members of Council, the said house shall nominate ten persons qualified as aforesaid, and return their names to Congress, five of whom Congress shall appoint and commission to serve as Members of the council five years, unless sooner removed. And the Governor, legislative council, and house of representatives, shall have authority to make laws in all cases for the good government of the district, not repugnant to the principles and Articles in this Ordinance established and declared. And all bills having passed by a majority in the house, and by a majority in the council, shall be referred to the Governor for his assent; but no bill or legislative Act whatever, shall be of any force without his assent. The Governor shall have power to convene, prorogue and dissolve the General Assembly, when in his opinion it shall be expedient.

The Governor, Judges, legislative Council, Secretary, and such other Officers as Congress shall appoint in the district shall take an

Oath or Affirmation of fidelity, and of Office, the Governor before the president of Congress, and all other Officers before the Governor. As soon as a legislature shall be formed in the district, the Council and house assembled in one room, shall have authority by joint ballot to elect a Delegate to Congress, who shall have a seat in Congress, with a right of debating, but not of voting, during this temporary Government.

And for extending the fundamental principles of civil and religious liberty, which form the basis whereon these republics, their laws and constitutions are erected; to fix and establish those principles as the basis of all laws, constitutions and governments, which forever hereafter shall be formed in the said territory; to provide also for the establishment of States and permanent government therein, and for their admission to a share in the federal Councils on an equal footing with the original States, at as early periods as may be consistent with the general interest,

It is hereby Ordained and declared by the authority aforesaid, That the following Articles shall be considered as Articles of compact between the Original States and the people and States in the said territory, and forever remain unalterable, unless by common consent, *to wit,*

Article the First. No person demeaning himself in a peaceable and orderly manner shall ever be molested on account of his mode of worship or religious sentiments in the said territory.

Article the Second. The Inhabitants of the said territory shall always be entitled to the benefits of the writ of habeas corpus, and of the trial by Jury; of a proportionate representation of the people in the legislature, and of judicial proceedings according to the course of the common law; all persons shall be bailable unless for capital offenses, where the proof shall be evident, or the presumption great; all fines shall be moderate, and no cruel or unusual punishments shall be inflicted; no man shall be deprived of his liberty or property but by the judgment of his peers, or the law of the land; and should the public exigencies make it necessary for the common preservation to take any persons property, or to demand his particular services, full compensation shall be made for the same; and in the just preservation of rights and property it is understood and declared; that no law ought ever to be made, or have force in the said territory, that shall in any manner whatever interfere with, or affect private contracts or engagements, bona fide and without fraud previously formed.

Article the Third. Religion, Morality and knowledge being necessary to good government and the happiness of mankind, Schools and the means of education shall forever be encouraged. The utmost good faith shall always be observed towards the Indians, their lands and property shall never be taken from them without their consent; and in their property, rights and liberty, they never shall be invaded or disturbed, unless in just and lawful wars authorised by Congress; but laws founded in justice and humanity shall from time to time be made, for preventing wrongs being done to them, and for preserving peace and friendship with them.

Article the Fourth. The said territory, and the States which may be formed therein shall forever remain a part of this Confederacy of the United States of America, subject to the Articles of Confederation, and to such alterations therein as shall be constitutionally made; and to all the Acts and Ordinances of the United States in Congress Assembled, conformable thereto. The Inhabitants and Settlers in the said territory, shall be subject to pay a part of the federal debts contracted or to be contracted, and a proportional part of the expences of Government, to be apportioned on them by Congress, according to the same common rule and measure by which apportionments thereof shall be made on the other States; and the taxes for paying their proportion, shall be laid and levied by the authority and direction of the legislatures of the district or districts or new States, as in the original States, within the time agreed upon by the United States in Congress Assembled. The Legislatures of those districts, or new States, shall never interfere with the primary disposal of the Soil by the United States in Congress Assembled, nor with any regulations Congress may find necessary for securing the title in such soil to the bona fide purchasers. No tax shall be imposed on lands the property of the United States; and in no case shall non resident proprietors be taxed higher than residents. The navigable Waters leading into the Missisippi and St. Lawrence, and the carrying places between the same shall be common highways, and forever free, as well to the Inhabitants of the said territory, as to the Citizens of the United States, and those of any other States that may be admitted into the Confederacy, without any tax, impost or duty therefor.

Article the Fifth. There shall be formed in the said territory, not less than three nor more than five States, and the boundaries of the States, as soon as Virginia shall alter her act of cession and consent to the same, shall become fixed and established as follows, to wit: The Western State in the said territory, shall be bounded by the Missisippi, the Ohio and Wabash Rivers; a direct line drawn from the Wabash and post Vincents due North to the territorial line between the United States and Canada, and by the said territorial line to the lake of the Woods and Missisippi. The middle State shall be bounded by the said direct line, the Wabash from post Vincents to the Ohio; by the Ohio, by direct line drawn due North from the mouth of the great Miami to the said territorial line, and by the said territorial line. The eastern State shall be bounded by the last mentioned direct line, the Ohio, Pensylvania, and the said territorial line; provided however, and it is further understood and declared, that the boundaries of these three States, shall be subject so far to be altered, that if Congress shall hereafter find it expedient, they shall have authority to form one or two States in that part of the said territory which lies north of an east and west line drawn through the southerly bend or extreme of lake Michigan; and whenever any of the said States shall have sixty thousand free Inhabitants therein, such State shall be admitted by its Delegates into the Congress of the United States, on an equal footing with the original States, in all respects whatever; and shall be at liberty to form a permanent constitution and State government, provided the constitution and government so to be formed, shall be republican, and in conformity to the principles contained in these Articles; and so far as it can be consistent with the general interest of the Confederacy, such admission shall be allowed at an earlier period, and when there may be a less number of free Inhabitants in the State than sixty thousand.

Article the Sixth. There shall be neither Slavery nor involuntary Servitude in the said territory otherwise than in the punishment of crimes, whereof the party shall have been duly convicted; provided always that any person escaping into the same, from whom labor or service is lawfully claimed in any one of the original States, such fugitive may be lawfully reclaimed and conveyed to the person claiming his or her labor or service as aforesaid.

Be it Ordained by the Authority aforesaid, that the Resolutions of the 23d of April 1784 relative to the subject of this ordinance be, and the same are hereby repealed and declared null and void.

Done &c.

ACT CREATING INDIANA TERRITORY, 1800

On March 20, 1800, a bill was introduced in the House of Representatives providing for the division of the Northwest Territory into two separate governments. It passed the House on March 31 and the Senate on April 21 in an amended form. After agreement had been achieved in a conference committee, it was approved by President John Adams on May 7, 1800. The principal supporters of the measure were William Henry Harrison, territorial delegate from Northwest Territory, and Robert G. Harper of South Carolina. They urged that the existing situation was too unwieldy for good government, that the growth of population justified the change, and that popular sentiment made it highly desirable. The passage of this act left the present state of Ohio, approximately half of Michigan and the "gore" in southeastern Indiana in the Northwest Territory and constituted the remainder of the original Northwest Territory as Indiana Territory:[13]

An ACT *to divide the territory of the United States north-west of the Ohio, into two separate governments.*

Sec. 1.   Be *it enacted by the Senate and House of Representatives of the United States of America, in Congress assembled,* That from and after the fourth day of July next, all that part of the territory of the United States north-west of the Ohio river, which lies to the westward of a line beginning at the Ohio, opposite to the mouth of Kentucky river, and running thence to fort Recovery, and thence north until it shall intersect the territorial line between the United States and Canada, shall, for the purposes of temporary government, constitute a separate territory, and be called the Indiana Territory.

Sec. 2.   *And be it further enacted,* That there shall be established within the said territory a government in all respects similar to that provided by the ordinance of Congress, passed on the thirteenth day of July one thousand seven hundred and eighty-seven, for the government of the territory of the United States north-west of the river Ohio; and the inhabitants thereof shall be entitled to, and enjoy all and singular the rights, privileges and advantages granted and secured to the people by the said ordinance.

---

[13] *Acts Passed at the First Session of the Sixth Congress of the United States* (Philalelphia. n.d.), 139-141; *United States Statutes at Large* (Boston, 1850-), II, 58-60; *Annals of Congress,* 6 Cong., 1 Sess., 645, 649, 1498-1500; Carter (ed.), *Territorial Papers,* VII, 7-10; Kettleborough (ed.), *Constitution Making in Indiana,* I, 39-43; Barnhart and Carmony, *Indiana,* I, 94-95, 100. The "gore" was transferred to Indiana Territory when Ohio became a state in 1803.

Sec. 3. *And be it further enacted,* That the officers for the said territory, who by virtue of this act shall be appointed by the President of the United States, by and with the advice and consent of the Senate, shall respectively exercise the same powers, perform the same duties, and receive for their services the same compensations as by the ordinance aforesaid and the laws of the United States, have been provided and established for similar officers in the territory of the United States north-west of the river Ohio: And the duties and emoluments of Superintendant of Indian Affairs shall be united with those of governor: *Provided,* That the President of the United States shall have full power, in the recess of Congress, to appoint and commission all officers herein authorized; and their commissions shall continue in force until the end of the next session of Congress.

Sec. 4. *And be it further enacted,* That so much of the ordinance for the government of the territory of the United States northwest of the Ohio river, as relates to the organization of a General Assembly therein, and prescribes the powers thereof, shall be in force and operate in the Indiana territory, whenever satisfactory evidence shall be given to the governor thereof, that such is the wish of a majority of the free-holders, notwithstanding there may not be therein five thousand free male inhabitants of the age of twenty-one years and upwards: *Provided,* That until there shall be five thousand free male inhabitants of twenty-one years and upwards in said territory, the whole number of representatives to the General Assembly shall not be less than seven, nor more than nine, to be apportioned by the governor to the several counties in the said territory, agreeably to the number of free males of the age of twenty-one years and upwards which they may respectively contain.

Sec. 5. *And be it further enacted,* That nothing in this act contained shall be construed so as in any manner to affect the government now in force in the territory of the United States north-west of the Ohio river, further than to prohibit the exercise thereof within the Indiana territory, from and after the aforesaid fourth day of July next: *Provided,* That whenever that part of the territory of the United States which lies to the eastward of a line beginning at the mouth of the Great Miami river, and running thence due north to the territorial line between the United States and Canada, shall be erected into an independent state, and admitted into the Union on an equal footing with the original states, thenceforth said line shall become and remain permanently the boundary line between such state and the Indiana territory; any thing in this act contained to the contrary notwithstanding.

Sec. 6. *And be it further enacted,* That until it shall be otherwise ordered by the legislatures of the said territories respectively, Chilicothe, on Scioto river, shall be the seat of the government of the territory of the United States north-west of the Ohio river; and that Saint Vincennes, on the Wabash river, shall be the seat of the government for the Indiana territory.

THEODORE SEDGWICK,
Speaker of the House of Representatives.

TH: JEFFERSON,
Vice-President of the United States, and President of the Senate.

Approved—May 7th, A. D. 1800

JOHN ADAMS, *President of the United States.*

HARRISON LAND ACT, 1800

Harrison was also concerned about the availability of land to actual settlers rather than speculative purchasers. The sale provisions of the Northwest Ordinance had been altered by the Land Act of 1796 when the minimum price was doubled. The difficulty of getting a farm at a price they could afford to pay led many to become squatters on the public domain with no legal title. Harrison's Land Act of 1800 reduced the minimum amount that might be purchased from 640 acres to 320 and introduced a credit feature. One-fourth of the price was required at purchase and the balance in installments within four years with an additional year to make up arrears. The minimum price was unchanged. This brought land within the reach of at least a large portion of those desiring to settle in the Northwest. The Land Act of 1804 reduced the minimum amount to 160 acres. The credit provision worked badly in terms of government revenue and was eventually repealed in 1820.[14]

An ACT *to amend the act, intituled, "An act providing for the sale of the lands of the United States, in the territory north-west of the Ohio, and above the mouth of Kentucky river."*

Sec. 1. Be *it enacted by the Senate and House of Representatives of the United States of America, in Congress assembled,* That for the disposal of the lands of the United States, directed to be sold by the act, intituled, "An act providing for the sale of the lands of the United States, in the territory north-west of the Ohio, and above the mouth of Kentucky river," there shall be four land-offices established in the said territory: One at Cincinnati, for lands below the Little Miami which have not heretofore been granted; one at Chilicothe, for lands east of the Sciota, south of the lands appropriated for satisfying military bounties to the late army of the United States, and west of the fifteenth range of townships; one at Marietta, for the lands east of the sixteenth range of townships, south of the before-mentioned military lands, and south of a line drawn due west from the north-west corner of the first township of the second range, to the said military lands; and one at Steubenville, for the lands north of the last mentioned line, and east or north of the said military lands: Each of

---

[14] *Acts Passed at the First Session of the 6th Congress of the United States,* 174-187; *U. S. Statutes at Large,* II, 73-78; *Annals of Congress,* 6 Cong., 1 Sess., 625, 660, 680-83; Carter (ed.), *Territorial Papers,* III, 88-97; Bond, *Civilization of the Old Northwest,* 282-286, 293-94; R. C. Buley, *The Old Northwest: Pioneer Period, 1815-1840* (2 vols., Indianapolis, 1950), I, 102-104; Barnhart and Carmony, *Indiana,* I, 93-94.

the said offices shall be under the direction of an officer, to be called "The Register of the Land-Office," who shall be appointed by the President of the United States, by and with the advice and consent of the Senate, and shall give bond to the United States, with approved security, in the sum of ten thousand dollars, for the faithful discharge of the duties of his office; and shall reside at the place where the land-office is directed to be kept.

Sec. 2. *And be it further enacted,* That it shall be the duty of the Surveyor-General, and he is hereby expressly enjoined, to prepare and transmit to the Registers of the several land-offices, before the days herein appointed for commencing sales, general plats of the lands hereby directed to be sold at the said offices respectively, and also to forward copies of each of the said plats to the Secretary of the Treasury.

Sec. 3. *And be it further enacted,* That the Surveyor-General shall cause the townships west of the Muskingum, which by the above-mentioned act are directed to be sold in quarter townships, to be sub-divided into half sections of three hundred and twenty acres each, as nearly as may be, by running parallel lines through the same from east to west, and from south to north, at the distance of one mile from each other, and marking corners, at the distance of each half mile on the lines running from east to west, and at the distance of each mile on those running from south to north, and making the marks, notes, and descriptions, prescribed to surveyors by the above-mentioned act: And the interior lines of townships intersected by the Muskingum, and of all the townships lying east of that river, which have not been heretofore actually sub-divided into sections, shall also be run and marked in the manner prescribed by the said act, for running and marking the interior lines of townships directed to be sold in sections of six hundred and forty acres each: And in all cases where the exterior lines of the townships, thus to be sub-divided into sections or half sections, shall exceed or shall not extend six miles, the excess or deficiency shall be specially noted, and added to or deducted from the western and northern ranges of sections or half sections in such township, according as the error may be in running the lines from east to west, or from south to north; the sections and half sections bounded on the northern and western lines of such townships shall be sold as containing only the quantity expressed in the returns and plats respectively, and all others as containing the complete legal quantity: And the President of the United States shall fix the compensation of the deputy-surveyors, chain-carriers, and axemen: *Provided,* the whole expense of surveying and marking the lines shall not exceed three dollars, for every mile that shall be actually run, surveyed and marked.

Sec. 4. *And be it further enacted,* That the lands thus subdivided (excluding the sections reserved by the above-mentioned act) shall be offered for sale in sections and half sections, sub-divided as before directed at the following places and times, that is to say; those below the Little Miami shall be offered at public vendue, in the town of Cincinnati, on the first Monday of April one thousand eight hundred and one, under the direction of the Register of the land-office there established, and of either the Governor or Secretary of the north-western territory: The lands east of Sciota, south of the military lands, and west of the fifteenth range of townships, shall be offered in like manner for the sale at Chilicothe, on the first Monday of May, one thousand eight hundred and one, under the direction of the Register of the land-office there established, and of either the Governor or Secretary of the said territory: The lands east of the sixteenth range of townships, south of the military lands and west of the Muskingum, including all the townships intersected by that river, shall be offered for sale in like manner at Marietta, on the last Monday of May, one thousand eight hundred and one, under the direction of the Governor or Secretary, or Surveyor-General of the said territory. The sales shall remain open at each place for three weeks and no longer. The superintendants shall observe the rules and regulations of the above-mentioned act, in classing and selling fractional with entire sections, and in keeping and transmitting accounts of the sales. All lands, remaining unsold, at the closing of either of the public sales, may be disposed of at private sale by the Registers of these respective land-offices, in the manner herein after prescribed; and the Register of the land-office at Steubenville, after the first day of July next, may proceed to sell at private sale, the lands situate within the district assigned to his direction as herein before described, disposing of the same in sections, and classing fractional with entire sections, according to the provisions and regulations of the above-mentioned act and of this act: And the Register of the land-office at Marietta, after the said first day of July next, may proceed to sell at private sale, any of the lands within the district assigned to his direction as aforesaid, which are east of the river Muskingum, excluding the townships intersected by that river, disposing of the same in sections, and classing fractional with entire sections as aforesaid.

Sec. 5. *And be it further enacted,* That no lands shall be sold by virtue of this act, at either public or private sale, for less than two dollars per acre, and payment may be made for the same by all purchasers, either in specie, or in evidences of the public debt of the United States, at the rates prescribed by the act, intituled, "An act to authorize the receipt of evidences of the public debt in payment for the lands of the United States;" and shall be made in the following manner, and under the following conditions, to wit:

1. At the time of purchase, every purchaser shall, exclusively of the fees hereinafter-mentioned, pay six dollars for every section, and three dollars for every half section, he may have purchased, for surveying expenses, and deposit one-twentieth part of the amount of the purchase money, to be forfeited, if within forty days one fourth part of the purchase money, including the said twentieth part, is not paid.

2. One-fourth part of the purchase money shall be paid within forty days after the day of sale as aforesaid; another fourth part shall be paid within two years; another fourth part within three years; and another fourth part within four years after the day of sale.

3. Interest, at the rate of six per cent. a year, from the day of sale, shall be charged upon each of the three last payments, payable as they respectively become due.

4. A discount, at the rate of eight per cent. a year, shall be allowed on any of the three last payments, which shall be paid before the same shall become due, reckoning this discount always upon the sum, which would have been demandable by the United States, on the day appointed for such payment.

5. If the first payment of one fourth part of the purchase money shall not be made within forty days after the sale, the deposit, payment and fees, paid and made by the purchaser, shall be forfeited, and the lands shall and may, from and after the day, when the pay-

ment of one fourth part of the purchase money should have been made, be disposed of at private sale, on the same terms and conditions, and in the same manner as the other lands directed by this act to be disposed of at private sale: *Provided,* That the lands which shall have been sold at public sale, and which shall, on account of such failure of payment, revert to the United States, shall not be sold at private sale, for a price less than the price that shall have been offered for the same at public sale.

6. If any tract shall not be completely paid for within one year after the date of the last payment, the tract shall be advertised for sale by the Register of the land-office within whose district it may lie, in at least five of the most public places in the said district, for at least thirty days before the time of sale: And he shall sell the same at public vendue, during the sitting of the court of quarter sessions of the county in which the land-office is kept, for a price not less than the whole arrears due thereon, with the expenses of sale; the surplus, if any, shall be returned to the original purchaser, or to his legal representative; but if the sum due, with interest, be not bidden and paid, then the land shall revert to the United States. All monies paid therefor shall be forfeited, and the Register of the land-office may proceed to dispose of the same to any purchaser, as in case of other lands at private sale.

Sec. 6. *And be it further enacted,* That all and every the payments, to be made by virtue of the preceding section, shall be made either to the Treasurer of the United States, or to such person or officer as shall be appointed by the President of the United States, with the advice and consent of the Senate, Receiver of public monies for lands of the United States, at each of the places respectively where the public and private sales of the said lands are to be made; and the said Receiver of public monies shall, before he enters upon the duties of his office, give bond, with approved security, in the sum of ten thousand dollars, for the faithful discharge of his trust; and it shall be the duty of the said Treasurer and Receiver of public monies to give receipts for the monies by them received, to the persons respectively paying the same; to transmit within thirty days in case of public sale, and quarterly in case of private sale, an account of all the public monies by them received, specifying the amount received from each person, and distinguishing the sums received from surveying expenses, and those received for purchase money, to the Secretary of the Treasury, and to the Registers of the land-office, as the case may be. The said Receivers of public monies shall, within three months after receiving the same, transmit the monies by them received to the Treasurer of the United States; and the Receivers of public monies for the said sales, and also the Receivers of public monies for the sales which have taken place at Pittsburg under the act, intituled, "An act providing for the sale of the lands of the United States in the territory north-west of the Ohio, and above the mouth of Kentucky river," shall receive one per cent. on the money received, as a compensation for clerk hire, receiving, safe-keeping, and transmitting it to the Treasury of the United States.

Sec. 7. *And be it further enacted,* That it shall be the duty of the Registers of the land-offices respectively, to receive and enter on books kept for that purpose only, and on which no blank leaves or space shall be left between the different entries, the applications of any person or persons who may apply for the purchase of any section or half section, and who shall pay him the fee hereafter-mentioned, and produce a receipt from the Treasurer of the United States, or from the Receiver of public monies appointed for that purpose, for three dollars for each half section such person or persons may apply for, and for at least one-twentieth part of the purchase money, stating carefully in each entry the date of the application, the date of the receipt to him produced, the amount of monies specified in the said receipt, and the number of the section or half section, township and range applied for. If two or more persons shall apply at the same time for the said tract, the Register shall immediately determine by lot, in presence of the parties, which of them shall have preference. He shall file the receipt for monies produced by the party, and give him a copy of his entry, and if required, a copy of the description of the tract, and a copy of the plat of the same, or either of them; and it shall be his duty to inform the party applying for any one tract, whether the same has already been entered, purchased, or paid for, and at his request to give him a copy of the entry or entries concerning the same. He shall, three months after the date of each application, if the party shall not have within that time produced to him a receipt of the payment of one fourth part of the purchase money, including the twentieth part above-mentioned, enter under its proper date, in the said book of entries, that the payment has not been made, and that the land has reverted to the United States, and he shall make a note of the same in the margin of the book opposite to the original entry. And if the party shall, either at the time of making the original entry, or at any time within three months thereafter, produce a receipt to him, for the fourth part of the purchase money, including the twentieth part aforesaid, he shall file the receipt, make an entry of the same, under its proper date, in the said book of entries, make a note of the same in the margin of the book, opposite to the original entry, and give to the party a certificate, describing the land sold, the sum paid on account, the balance remaining due, the time and times when such balance shall become due, and that if it shall be duly discharged, the purchaser or his assignee or other legal representative, shall be entitled to a patent for the said lands; he shall also upon any subsequent payment being made, and a receipt from the receiver being produced to him, file the original receipt, give a receipt for the same to the party, and enter the same to the credit of the party, in a book kept for that purpose, in which he shall open an account in the name of each purchaser, for each section or half section that may be sold either at public or private sale, and in which he shall charge the party for the whole purchase money, and give him credit for all his payments; making the proper charges and allowances for interest or discount, as the case may be, according to the provisions of the fourth section of this act; and upon the payment being completed and the account finally settled, he shall give a certificate of the same to the party; and on producing to the Secretary of the Treasury, the same final certificate, the President of the United States is hereby authorized to grant a patent for the lands to the said purchaser, his heirs or assigns; and all patents shall be countersigned by the Secretary of State, and recorded in his office.

Sec. 8. *And be it further enacted,* That the Registers of the land-offices respectively, shall also note on the book of surveys, or original plat transmitted to them, every tract which may be sold, by inserting the letter A on the day when the same is applied for, and the letter P on the day when a receipt for one fourth part of the purchase money is produced to them, and by crossing the said letter A on the day when the land shall revert to the United States, on failure of the payment of one fourth part of the purchase money within three months after the date of application. And the said book of surveys or original plat shall be open at all times, in presence of the Register, for the inspection of any individual, applying for the same and paying the proper fee.

Sec. 9. *And be it further enacted,* That it shall be the duty of the Registers of the land-offices to transmit quarterly to the Secretary of the Treasury, and to the Surveyor-General, an account of the several tracts applied for, of the several tracts for which the payment of one fourth part of the purchase money has been made, of the several tracts which have reverted to the United States on failure of the said payment; and also an account of all the payments of monies by them entered, according to the receipts produced to them, specifying the sums of money, the names of the persons paying the same, the names of the officers who have received the same, and the tracts for which the same have been paid.

Sec. 10. *And be it further enacted,* That the Registers aforesaid shall be precluded from entering on their books any application for lands in their own name, and in the name of any other person in trust for them; and if any Register shall wish to purchase any tract of land, he may do it by application in writing to the Surveyor-General, who shall enter the same on books kept for that purpose by him, who shall proceed in respect to such applications, and to any payments made for the same, in the same manner which the Registers by this act are directed to follow, in respect to applications made to them for lands by other persons. The Registers shall, nevertheless, note on the book of surveys, or original plat, the applications and payments thus by them made, and their right to the pre-emption of any tract shall bear date from the day, when their application for the same shall have been entered by the Surveyor-General in his own book. And if any person applying for any tract shall, not withstanding he shall have received information from the Register, that the same has already been applied for by the said Register, or by any other person, insist to make the application, it shall be the duty of the Register to enter the same, noting in the margin that the same tract is already purchased; but upon application of the party made in writing, and which he shall file, he may and shall at any future time enter under its proper date, that the party withdraws his former application, and applies in lieu thereof for any other tract: *Provided always,*

That the party shall never be allowed thus to withdraw his former application, and to apply in lieu thereof for another tract, except when the tract described in his former application shall have been applied for previous to the date of that his former application.

Sec. 11. *And be it further enacted,* That the Secretary of the Treasury shall and may prescribe such further regulations, in the manner of keeping books and accounts, by the several officers in this act mentioned, as to him may appear necessary and proper, in order fully to carry into effect the provisions of this act.

Sec. 12. *And be it further enacted,* That the Registers of the land-offices, respectively, shall be entitled to receive from the Treasury of the United States, one-half per cent. on all the monies expressed in the receipts by them filed and entered, and of which they shall have transmitted an account to the Secretary of the Treasury, as directed by this act; and they shall further be entitled to receive, for their own use, from the respective parties, the following fees for services rendered, that is to say; for every original application for land, and a copy of the same, for a section three dollars, for a half section two dollars, for every certificate stating that the first fourth part of the purchase money is paid, twenty-five cents; for every subsequent receipt for monies paid, twenty-five cents; for the final settlement of account and giving the final certificate of the same, one dollar; for every copy, either of an application or of the description of any section or half section, or of the plat of the same, or of any entry made on their books, or of any certificate heretofore given by them, twenty-five cents for each; and for any general inspection of the book of surveys, or general plat, made in their presence, twenty-five cents.

Sec. 13. *And be it further enacted,* That the superintendants of the public sales, to be made by virtue of this act, and the superintendants of the sales which have taken place by virtue of the act, intituled, "An act providing for the sale of the lands of the United States in the territory north-west of the river Ohio, and above the mouth of Kentucky river," shall receive five dollars a day for every day whilst engaged in that business; and the accounting officers of the Treasury are hereby authorized to allow a reasonable compensation for books, stationery, and clerk hire, in settling the accounts of the said superintendants.

Sec. 14. *And be it further enacted,* That the fee to be paid for each patent for half a section shall be four dollars, and for every section five dollars, to be accounted for by the receiver of the same.

Sec. 15. *And be it further enacted,* That the lands of the United States reserved for future disposition, may be let upon leases by the Surveyor-General, in sections or half sections, for terms not exceeding seven years, on condition of making such improvements as he shall deem reasonable.

Sec. 16. *And be it further enacted,* That each person who before the passing of this act shall have erected, or begun to erect, a grist-mill or saw-mill upon any of the lands herein directed to be sold, shall be entitled to the pre-emption of the section including such mill, at the rate of two dollars per acre: *Provided,* The person or his heirs, claiming such right of pre-emption, shall produce to the Register of the land-office satisfactory evidence that he or they are entitled thereto, and shall be subject to and comply with the regulations and provisions by this act prescribed for other purchasers.

Sec. 17. *And be it further enacted,* That so much of the "act providing for the sale of the lands of the United States in the territory north-west of the river Ohio, and above the mouth of Kentucky river," as comes within the purview of this act, be and the same is hereby repealed.

THEODORE SEDGWICK,
Speaker of the House of Representatives.

TH: JEFFERSON,
*Vice-President of the United States, and
President of the Senate.*

Approved—May 10th, A. D. 1800.

JOHN ADAMS,
President of the United States.

PROCLAMATION: FOR AN ELECTION ON
ENTERING SECOND TERRITORIAL STAGE

In August, 1804, Governor Harrison issued a proclamation calling for an election to determine the will of the freeholders in Indiana Territory regarding the organization of a general assembly. He had opposed demands for an advance to the second territorial stage in 1801 but gave the movement his support in 1804. The three counties of Indiana Territory located in the future state of Indiana were Knox, Dearborn, and Clark. They cast 51 votes opposing the advance and 198 favoring it.[15]

August 4, 1804

Vincennes *Indiana Gazette,* August 21, 1804

Whereas, By a Law of the United States entitled "An act to divide the Territory of the United States North West of the Ohio, into two seperate Governments," it is enacted and declared "that so much of the ordinance for government of the Territory of the United States North West of the Ohio river as relates to the organization of a general assembly therein, and prescribes the powers thereof, shall be in force and operate in the Indiana Territory, whenever satisfactory evidence shall be given to the governor thereof that such is the wish of the majority of the freeholders, notwithstanding there may not be five thousand free male inhabitants of the age of twenty-one years and upward";

And *whereas,* Petitions have been presented to me from a number of the good citizens of the Territory praying that a General Assembly may be organized, conformably to the above recited act, but as no evidence has been adduced to shew that the persons who have signed the said petitions are really a majority of the freeholders:

Now *therefore,* for the purpose of ascertaining more correctly the public sentiment on the subject, I have thought proper to issue this my proclamation hereby making known to all whom it may concern that an election will be held at the court house of each county

---

[15] Vincennes *Indiana Gazette,* August 21, 1804, in Logan Esarey (ed.), *Messages and Letters of William Henry Harrison* (2 vols., *Indiana Historical Collections,* VII, IX, Indianapolis, 1922), I, 106-07; Dorothy B. Goebel, *William Henry Harrison: A Political Biography* (*Indiana Historical Collections,* XIV, Indianapolis, 1926), 78-79; Barnhart and Carmony, *Indiana,* I, 107-09; Dunn, *Indiana and Indianans,* I, 228, 240-41.

respectively on Tuesday the eleventh day of September next, for the purpose of giving to all the citizens of the Territory who are qualified by law to vote on the question of going into the second or representative grade of government, an opportunity of declaring their wishes on the subject. And it is hereby made the duty of the several sheriffs to give due notice of the same, and on the said eleventh of September to open polls at the several court houses of their respective counties for the purpose aforesaid; and the said election shall be conducted in the same manner and governed by the same principles as are laid down in a law regulating the elections of representatives for the General Assembly of the North Western Territory passed at Cincinnati, the 6th of December, 1799.

In testimony whereof, I have hereunto set my hand and caused the seal of the Territory to be affixed at Vincennes, the fourth day of August in the year of our Lord one thousand eight hundred and four, and of the Independence of the United States the twenty-ninth.

WILLIAM HENRY HARRISON

By the Governor:

JOHN GIBSON, *Secretary*.

PROCLAMATION: ANNOUNCING THAT INDIANA TERRITORY HAD PASSED TO THE SECOND GRADE

On December 5, 1804, Harrison proclaimed Indiana Territory's advance to the "second or representative grade of Government":[16]

December 5, 1804

Executive Journal, 11

Returns of the Election held on the 11th Sept. last in the several Counties, having been made to the office of the Secretary of the Territory (that of the County of Wayne excepted in which there was no Election in Consequence of the proclamation not arriving in time), and [it] appearing that there was a majority of one hundred and thirty Eight Freeholders in favor of the proposed Change of Government, the Governor Issued a proclamation in which he makes known and Declares the said Indiana Territory is and from henceforth shall be deemed to have passed into the second or representative grade of Government, and that the Good people of the Territory, from the date thereof are entitled to all the rights and privileges belonging to that situation, and further appoints that on Thursday the third day of January next an Election shall be held in each of the several Counties in the Territory respectively for the purpose of choosing the members of the house of Representatives and that the said house of representatives shall be composed of nine members of which there shall be Elected from the County of Knox Two from the County St. Clair one from the County of Randolph one from the County of Clark one from the County of Wayne three & from the County of Dearborn one, and that the said representatives Elected and every of them should meet at the Town of Vincennes on the first day of February next for the purpose of choosing members for the Legislative Council agreeable to the ordinance for the Government of the Territory.

---

[16] Esarey, *Messages and Letters of Harrison*, I, 112-13.

PETITION TO CONGRESS BY DEMOCRATIC REPUBLICANS OF WAYNE COUNTY

Settlements in distant portions of Indiana Territory suffered serious inconvenience and, on occasion, pecuniary loss because of difficulties of travel and communication. As indicated in Harrison's Proclamation of December 5, 1804, residents of Wayne County (Michigan) had been unable to participate in the voting on advancing to the second grade "in Consequence of the proclamation not arriving in time." The following petition from Wayne County shows their strong desire for a separate territorial government:[17]

[Referred *December* 6, 1804]

The Senate and House of Representatives of the United States in Congress Assembled

The *Democratic Republicans* of the County of *Wayne* in the Territory of *Indiana,* come *collectively* forward for the *first time,* in order to state to Congress, the situation and the wishes of these frontier Settlements.—

We ask of Congress a Division of the Indiana territory,—and a separate local government for those Settlements, which at this time compose the County of Wayne; whose southern boundary shall be, a line drawn from the southern extremity of Lake Michigan in such a south easterly direction, until it meets the western boundary of the State of Ohio, or Lake Erie, as to include within said local government, the small settlements at the old forts Defiance, and Miamis, and also all the settlements on, and adjacent to River Raisin.

Not, that we would be obstinately troublesome, in the repetition of requests, which have been once denied us—but subjected as we have been, to a variety of embarrassments arising naturally out of our present organization, we are induced to believe, that Congress will, without reluctance, give their attention to the reconsideration of our claims, founded, as we conceive in justice and in policy.—

Suffer us to entreat you, to have justice promptly and impartially administered: compel us not to wander seven hundred miles, thro' inhospitable deserts, for the redress of wrongs, which the uncertainty

---

[17] Carter (ed.), *Territorial Papers,* VII, 240-42; Barnhart and Carmony, *Indiana,* I, 110-11.

of punishment, and the hopes of impunity, have, perhaps in many instances caused us to suffer.—

Persons *capitally punishable,* are seldom prosecuted to convictions. They remain in confinement for the want of competent authority to try them, until they are forgotten, when, with the assistance of their associates in guilt, they break their bonds, and deride, from the opposite bank, the impotence of our Magistrates.—

In *civil matters* too, the delay and the expense are equally fatal.— During the last eight years, we have had but two Circuit Courts.— The Creditor is deterred from an appeal to the laws, under the painful assurance, that altho' justice is not sold, it costs more than, some among us are, able to pay.—

These evils permit us to observe, will now be felt with accumulated weight, since the attention of our Governor and Judges, must now be shared with us by a large tract of additional Territory, annexed during your last session to the Indiana.

You know precisely our *situation,* our *Wants,* & our *necessities.* It will be unnecessary for us to repeat, with minutes, the arguments which were formerly detailed, in support of the justice, and the reasonableness of our pretensions.—

Our intercourse with Vincennes, *always* dilatory, circuitous and difficult, is now almost at an end, by a change in our Postrout to Warren in the State of Ohio. The people of Vincennes and of Detroit, governors and governed, as well as corresponding traders, can no longer rely on the mail conveyance, which must of necessity be substituted by expresses or by casual opportunities.

But at the same time that we remark this superadded difficulty in our correspondence with Vincennes, we must be permitted to express our obligations for a more ready ready [*sic*] and expeditious intercourse with the seat of the general government which this change will probably afford us.—

.   .   .   .

We patiently submit ourselves to your decision, whatever it may be, and desire you to be persuaded of our unlimited confidence.

ROBt ABBOTT
Chairman

Attest Go Hoffman Secretary

ACT DIVIDING INDIANA TERRITORY, 1805

In an act approved on January 11, 1805, Congress detached Wayne County from Indiana Territory and made it into the Michigan Territory:[18]

AN *ACT to divide the Indiana Territory into two separate governments.*

BE *it enacted, by the Senate and House of Representatives of the United States of America, in Congress assembled,* That from and after the thirtieth day of June next, all that part of the Indiana Territory, which lies North of a line drawn east from the southerly bend or extreme of lake Michigan, until it shall intersect lake Erie, and East of a line drawn from the said southerly bend through the middle of said lake to its northern extremity, and thence due north to the northern boundary of the United States, shall, for the purpose of temporary government, constitute a separate territory, and be called Michigan.

Sec. 2. *And be it further enacted,* That there shall be established within the said territory, a government in all respects similar to that provided by the ordinance of Congress, passed on the thirteenth day of July, one thousand seven hundred and eighty-seven, for the government of the territory of the United States, north west of the river Ohio; and by an act passed on the seventh day of August, one thousand seven hundred and eighty-nine, entitled "An act to provide for the government of the territory north west of the river Ohio;" and the inhabitants thereof shall be entitled to, and enjoy all and singular the rights, privileges, and advantages granted and secured to the people of the territory of the United States, north west of the river Ohio, by the said ordinance.

Sec. 3. *And be it further enacted,* That the officers for the said territory, who by virtue of this act shall be appointed by the President of the United States, by and with the advice and consent of the Senate, shall respectively exercise the same powers, perform the same duties, and receive for their services, the same compensations, as by

---

[18] *Acts Passed at the Second Session of the Eighth Congress of the United States* (Washington, 1805), 241-43; *U. S. Statutes at Large,* II, 309-310; Kettleborough (ed.), *Constitution Making in Indiana,* I, 43-47; Barnhart and Carmony, *Indiana,* I, 109.

the ordinance aforesaid and the laws of the United States, have been provided and established for similar officers in the Indiana Territory; and the duties and emoluments of superintendant of Indian affairs, shall be united with those of governor.

Sec. 4. *And be it further enacted,* That nothing in this act contained, shall be construed so as, in any manner, to affect the government now in force in the Indiana Territory, further than to prohibit the exercise thereof within the said territory of Michigan, from and after the aforesaid thirtieth day of June next.

Sec. 5. *And be it further enacted,* That all suits, process, and proceeding, which, on the thirtieth day of June next, shall be pending in the court of any county, which shall be included within the said territory of Michigan; and also all suits, process, and proceedings, which on the said thirtieth day of June next, shall be pending in the general court of the Indiana Territory, in consequence of any writ of removal, or order for trial at bar, and which had been removed from any of the counties included within the limits of the territory of Michigan aforesaid, shall, in all things concerning the same, be proceeded on, and judgments and decrees rendered thereon, in the same manner as if the said Indiana Territory had remained undivided.

Sec. 6. *And be it further enacted,* That Detroit shall be the seat of government of the said territory, until Congress shall otherwise direct.

NATH1. MACON,
Speaker of the House of Representatives.

A. BURR,
*Vice-President of the United States, and
President of the Senate.*

January 11, 1805.

Approved,
    TH: JEFFERSON.

THE TERRITORIAL LEGISLATURE TO THE PRESIDENT

The newly formed territorial legislature and President Thomas Jefferson exchanged epistolary courtesies in 1805. The communications suggest something of the contemporary importance attached to the legislative branch and self-government generally:[19]

[*August* 19, 1805]

To the President Of the United States.

Sir, At the auspicious moment which gives to the Indiana Territory a form of Government which bears some Semblance to a republic, the General Assembly thereof beg leave to Offer you their Congratulations on the prosperous and happy situation of the United States, under an Administration wise as it is virtuous, mild as it is energetic.

Although our peculiar Situation prevents our realizing the influence of all the measures of the Government of a general nature, yet we feel the firmest Conviction that your administration will eminently promote the happiness and prosperity of the Country over which you preside, And the advancement of the Cause of Republicanism throughout the world.

In taking a view of the Acts of the General Government, there Appears to be no one more interesting to the United States in general, and to the Western Country in particular, than the acquisition of Louisiana; whilst it has added an empire to the Union, it has secured to us the peace and friendship of the various Indian Tribes, and removed a danger Justly to be apprehended from its being possessed by a powerfull and ambitious European Nation: this Important transaction which has secured the Peace and happiness of Western America and the emancipation of Millions which are yet unborn, will for ever remain a monument at Once honourable to our Nation and to those who directed its negociation.

Accept, Sir, the thanks of the People of the Indiana territory for the attention you have paid to their particular interest, and their

---

[19] Carter (ed.), *Territorial Papers*, VII, 300, 329.

wishes that your domestic happiness may be as Complete as that which you have so ably Assisted to Secure to your fellow Citizens.

VINCENNES *August* 19th 1805.

B. CHAMBERS,
President of the Council

JESSE B. THOMAS Speaker
of the house of representatives

[*Endorsed*] Address Indiana. Genl Assembly. Chambers & Thomas Vincennes. Aug. 19. 05. recd Dec. 12.

THE PRESIDENT TO THE TERRITORIAL LEGISLATURE

[*December* 28, 1805]

To the President and legislative council, the Speaker & House of Representatives of the territory of Indiana.

I congratulate my fellow-citizens of Indiana, on the arrival of the auspicious moment which has entered them on the threshold of self-government, and placed within their early attainment all its valuable prerogatives. the sense their general assembly has expressed of the tendency of measures in which I have borne a part, to promote the cause of republicanism, assures me of their friendship to its principles & that their aid will never be wanting for its support.

The addition of a country so extensive, so fertile, as Louisiana, to the great republican family of this hemisphere, while it substitutes, for our neighbors, brethren & children in the place of strangers, has secured the blessings of civil & religious freedom to millions yet unborn. by enlarging the empire of liberty, we multiply its auxiliaries, & provide new sources of renovation, should its principles, at any time, degenerate, in those portions of our country which gave them birth. the securing for you the peace & friendship of the various Indian tribes is among the highly valued advantages of this acquisition.

The attentions to the interests of my Western brethren, which your address of Aug. 19. so kindly notices, having been acts of duty, have no other merit than the pleasure with which they were performed; and after returning my thanks to the General assembly of Indiana for the expressions of their good will, I tender them the homage of my high consideration & respect

TH: JEFFERSON

Washington *Dec.* 28. 1805.

THE SUFFRAGE ACT, 1808

Under the provisions of the Ordinance of 1787 a voter was required to be a free white male of twenty-one years or more, a resident of the district, and the owner of fifty acres of land in the district. The desire for a more liberal suffrage was apparent at an early date in Indiana Territory. Numerous petitions were submitted. In 1808 the Tenth Congress made a small but significant concession by extending the suffrage to those holding town lots with a minimum value of $100.00.[20]

AN ACT Extending the right of suffrage in the Indiana Territory. BE it enacted by the Senate and House of Representatives of the United States of America, in Congress assembled, That every free white male person in the Indiana territory, above the age of twenty-one years, having been a citizen of the United States, and resident in the said territory, one year next preceding an election of representatives, and who has a legal or equitable title to a tract of land of the quantity of fifty acres, or who may become the purchaser from the United States of a tract of land of the quantity of fifty acres, or who holds in his own right a town lot of the value of one hundred dollars, shall be entitled to vote for the representatives to the general assembly of the said territory.

J. B. VARNUM
Speaker of the House of Representatives.

GEO. CLINTON
Vice-President of the United States, and President of the Senate.

February 26, 1808.

APPROVED,
TH: JEFFERSON

---

[20] *The Laws of the United States of America: Acts Passed at the First Session of the Tenth Congress of the United States* (Washington, 1809), IX, 54-55; *U. S. Statutes at Large,* II, 469, cf. 525; *Annals of Congress,* 10 Cong., 1 Sess., 2834; Carter (ed.), *Territorial Papers,* VII, 526. For an excellent discussion of the democratic movement see John D. Barnhart, *Valley of Democracy: The Frontier versus the Plantation in the Ohio Valley, 1775-1818* (Bloomington, Indiana, 1953), 161-177.

ACT DIVIDING INDIANA TERRITORY, 1809

Congress received a number of petitions from Randolph and St. Clair Counties (in the present state of Illinois) urging a further division of Indiana Territory.[21] As in the earlier case of Wayne County (Michigan) the difficulties of travel and communication were cited, but, in addition, a resentment against Governor Harrison and a dislike of the second stage of territorial government are apparent.[22] Despite counter-petitions from Knox County, the Tenth Congress passed an act dividing Indiana Territory into two separate governments which was approved on February 3, 1809.[23]

AN ACT for dividing the Indiana Territory into two separate Governments.

Be it enacted, &c., That, from and after the first day of March next, all that part of the Indiana Territory which lies west of the Wabash river, and a direct line drawn from the said Wabash river and Post Vincennes, due north to the territorial line between the United States and Canada, shall, for the purpose of temporary government, constitute a separate Territory, and be called Illinois.

Sec. 2. *And be it further enacted,* That there shall be established within the said Territory a government in all respects similar to that provided by the ordinance of Congress, passed on the thirteenth day of July, one thousand seven hundred and eighty-seven, for the government of the Territory of the United States Northwest of the river Ohio; and by an act passed on the seventh day of August, one thousand seven hundred and eighty-nine, entitled "An act to provide for the government of the Territory Northwest of the river Ohio;" and the inhabitants thereof shall be entitled to, and enjoy all and singular the rights, privileges, and advantages, granted and secured to the people of the Territory of the United States Northwest of the river Ohio, by the said ordinance.

Sec. 3. *And be it further enacted,* That the officers for the

---

21 Carter (ed.), *Territorial Papers,* VII, 140-145, 544-554; Jacob P. Dunn, *Slavery Petitions and Papers* (Indiana Historical Society *Publications,* Vol. II, No. 12, Indianapolis, 1897), 483-491, 498-506, 510-512.
22 Carter (ed.), *Territorial Papers,* VII, 546-548.
23 *Annals of Congress,* 10 Cong., 2 Sess., 1808-1810; *Acts Passed at the Second Session of the Tenth Congress of the United States,* 208-211; *U. S. Statutes at Large,* II, 514-516; Carter (ed.), *Territorial Papers,* XVI, 6-8; Kettleborough (ed.), *Constitution Making in Indiana,* I, 54-56.

said Territory, who, by virtue of this act, shall be appointed by the President of the United States, by and with the advice and consent of the Senate, shall respectively exercise the same powers, perform the same duties, and receive for their services the same compensations as by the ordinance aforesaid, and the laws of the United States, have been provided and established for similar officers in the Indiana Territory. And the duties and emoluments of the Superintendent of Indian Affairs shall be united with those of Governor: *Provided,* That the President of the United States shall have full power, in the recess of Congress, to appoint and commission all officers herein authorized, and their commissions shall continue in force until the end of the next session of Congress.

Sec. 4. *And be it further enacted,* That so much of the ordinance for the government of the Territory of the United States Northwest of the Ohio river, as relates to the organization of a General Assembly therein, and prescribes the powers thereof, shall be in force, and operate in the Illinois Territory, whenever satisfactory evidence shall be given to the Governor thereof that such is the wish of a majority of the freeholders, notwithstanding there may not be therein five thousand free male inhabitants of the age of twenty-one years and upwards: *Provided,* That until there shall be five thousand free male inhabitants of twenty-one years and upwards in said Territory, the whole number of representatives to the General Assembly shall not be less than seven, nor more than nine, to be apportioned by the Governor to the several counties in the said Territory, agreeably to the number of free males of the age of twenty-one years and upwards, which they may respectively contain.

Sec. 5. *And be it further enacted,* That nothing in this act contained shall be construed so as in any manner to affect the government now in force in the Indiana Territory, further than to prohibit the exercise thereof within the Illinois Territory, from and after the aforesaid first day of March next.

Sec. 6. *And be it further enacted,* That all suits, process, and proceedings, which, on the first day of March next, shall be pending in the court of any county which shall be included within the said Territory of Illinois, and also all suits, process, and proceedings, which, on the said first day of March next, shall be pending in the general court of the Indiana Territory, in consequence of any writ of removal, or order for trial at bar, and which had been removed from any of the counties included within the limits of the Territory of Illinois aforesaid, shall, in all things concerning the same, be proceeded on, and judgments and decrees rendered thereon, in the same manner as if the said Indiana Territory had remained undivided.

Sec. 7. *And be it further enacted,* That nothing in this act contained shall be so construed as to prevent the collection of taxes which may, on the first day of March next, be due to the Indiana Territory on lands lying in the said Territory of Illinois.

Sec. 8. *And be it further enacted,* That until it shall be otherwise ordered by the Legislature of the said Illinois Territory, Kaskaskia, on the Mississippi river, shall be the seat of government for the said Illinois Territory.

Approved, February 3, 1809.

TREATY WITH THE DELAWARES, ETC., 1809

As Superintendent of Indian Affairs Governor Harrison enthusiastically implemented the aggressive policy of land acquisition authorized by the federal government. It was a case of hunting grounds versus cornfields. Indiana could not become a state so long as the Indians retained title. By a judicious mixture of persuasion and pressure Harrison secured the cession of approximately one-third of Indiana in a series of treaties from 1803 to 1809. In a treaty at Fort Wayne with "the Delawares, Putawatimies, Miamies, and Eel River Miamies" in the fall of 1809, he secured three million acres at an immediate cost of about one-third of a cent per acre. Indian opposition to cessions, led by Tecumseh and the Prophet, became increasingly bitter. As a result of the Treaty of 1809 Indian relations progressively deteriorated until Tecumseh's power was broken at the Battle of Tippecanoe.[24]

A treaty between the United States of America, and the tribes of Indians called the Delawares, Putawatimies, Miamies and Eel River Miamies.

JAMES MADISON, President of the United States, by William Henry Harrison, governor and commander-in-chief of the Indiana territory, superintendent of Indian affairs, and commissioner plenipotentiary of the United States for treating with the said Indian tribes, and the Sachems, Head men and Warriors of the Delaware, Putawatame, Miami and Eel River tribes of Indians, have agreed and concluded upon the following treaty; which, when ratified by the said President, with the advice and consent of the Senate of the United States, shall be binding on said parties.

ART. 1st. The Miami and Eel River tribes, and the Delawares and Putawatimies, as their allies, agree to cede to the United States all that tract of country which shall be included between the boundary line established by the treaty of Fort Wayne [1803], the Wabash, and a line to be drawn from the mouth of a creek called Racoon Creek, emptying into the Wabash, on the south-east side, about twelve miles below the mouth of the Vermilion river, so as to strike the boundary line established by the treaty of Grouseland, at such a distance from its commencement at the north-east corner of the Vin-

---

[24] Charles J. Kappler (ed.), *Indian Affairs: Laws and Treaties* (Washington, D. C., 1904), II, 101-102; *Laws of the United States*, X, 211-217, 192-194; Barnhart and Carmony, *Indiana*, I, 122-133.

cennes tract, as will leave the tract now ceded thirty miles wide at the narrowest place. And also all that tract which shall be included between the following boundaries, viz.: beginning at Fort Recovery, thence southwardly along the general boundary line, established by the treaty of Greenville, to its intersection with the boundary line established by the treaty of Grouseland; thence along said line to a point from which a line drawn parallel to the first mentioned line will be twelve miles distant from the same, and along the said parallel line to its intersection with a line to be drawn from Fort Recovery, parallel to the line established by the said treaty of Grouseland.

ART. 2d.   The Miamies explicitly acknowledge the equal right of the Delawares with themselves to the country watered by the White river. But it is also to be clearly understood that neither party shall have the right of disposing of the same without the consent of the other: and any improvements which shall be made on the said land by the Delawares, or their friends the Mochecans, shall be theirs forever.

ART. 3d.   The compensation to be given for the cession made in the first article shall be as follows, viz.: to the Delawares a permanent annuity of five hundred dollars; to the Miamies a like annuity of five hundred dollars; to the Eel river tribe a like annuity of two hundred and fifty dollars; and to the Putawatimies a like annuity of five hundred dollars.

ART. 4th.   All the stipulations made in the treaty of Greenville, relatively to the manner of paying the annuities, and the right of the Indians to hunt upon the land, shall apply to the annuities granted and the land ceded by the present treaty.

ART. 5th.   The consent of the Wea tribe shall be necessary to complete the title to the first tract of land here ceded; a separate convention shall be entered into between them and the United States, and a reasonable allowance of goods given them in hand, and a permanent annuity, which shall not be less than three hundred dollars, settled upon them.

ART. 6th.   The annuities promised by the third article, and the goods now delivered to the amount of five thousand two hundred dollars, shall be considered as a full compensation for the cession made in the first article.

ART. 7th.   The tribes who are parties to this treaty being desirous of putting an end to the depredations which are committed by abandoned individuals of their own color, upon the cattle, horses, &c. of the more industrious and careful, agree to adopt the following regulations, viz.: when any theft or other depredation shall be committed by any individual or individuals of one of the tribes above mentioned, upon the property of any individual or individuals of another tribe, the chiefs of the party injured shall make application to the agent of the United States, who is charged with the delivery of the annuities of the tribe to which the offending party belongs, whose duty it shall be to hear the proofs and allegations on either side, and determine between them: and the amount of his award shall be immediately deducted from the annuity of the tribe to which the offending party belongs, and given to the person injured, or to the chief of his village for his use.

ART. 8th.   The United States agree to relinquish their right to the reservation, at the old Ouroctenon towns, made by the treaty of Greenville, so far at least as to make no further use of it than for the establishment of a military post.

ART. 9th.   The tribes who are parties to this treaty, being desirous to show their attachment to their brothers the Kickapoos, agree to cede to the United States the lands on the north-west side of the Wabash, from the Vincennes tract to a northwardly extention of the line running from the mouth of the aforesaid Raccoon creek, and fifteen miles in width from the Wabash, on condition that the United States shall allow them an annuity of four hundred dollars. But this article is to have no effect unless the Kickapoos will agree to it.

In testimony whereof, the said William Henry Harrison, and the sachems and war chiefs of the beforementioned tribes, have hereunto set their hands and affixed their seals, at fort Wayne, this thirtieth of September, eighteen hundred and nine.

William Henry Harrison,		Mosser, his x mark,	(L.S.)
Delawares:	(L.S.)	Chequinimo, his x mark,	(L.S.)
Anderson, for Hocking-pomskon, who is absent,		Sackanackshut, his x mark,	(L.S.)

his x mark,   (L.S.)
Anderson, his x mark,   (L.S.)
Petchekekapon, his x
  mark,   (L.S.)
The Beaver, his x mark,   (L.S.)
Captain Killbuck, his x
  mark,   (L.S.)
  Pattawatimas:
Winemac, his x mark,   (L.S.)
Five Medals, by his son,
  his x mark,   (L.S.)
Mogawgo, his x mark,   (L.S.)
Shissahecon, for himself
  and his brother Tuthini-
  pee, his x mark,   (L.S.)
Ossmeet, brother to Five
  Medals, his x mark,   (L.S.)
Nanousekah, Penamo's
  son, his x mark,   (L.S.)

Conengee, his x mark,
  Miamis: (L.S.)
Pucan, his x mark,
The Owl, his x mark,   (L.S.)
Meshekenoghqua, or the
  Little Turtle, his x
  mark,   (L.S.)
Wapemangua, or the
  Loon, his x mark,   (L.S.)
Silver Heels, his x mark,   (L.S.)
Shawapenomo, his ex
  mark,
  Eel Rivers:
Charley, his x mark,   (L.S.)
Sheshangomequah, or
  Swallow, his x mark,   (L.S.)
The young Wyandot, a
  Miami of Elk Hart, his
  x mark,   (L.S.)

In presence of—

Peter Jones, secretary to the
  Commissioner,
John Johnson, Indian agent,
A. Heald, Capt. U. S. Army,
A. Edwards, surgeon's mate,
Ph. Ostrander, Lieut. U. S.
  Army,
John Shaw,

Stephen Johnston,
J. Hamilton, sheriff of Dearborn
  County,
Hendrick Aupaumut,
William Wells,
John Conner,
Joseph Barron,
Abraham Ash,
      Sworn Interpreters.

THE SUFFRAGE ACT, 1809

The qualifications for voting set by the Northwest Ordinance were liberalized by the act of February 26, 1808 (see above, p. 47). In an act of February 27, 1809, the qualified electors were authorized to select the congressional delegate and the members of the legislative council who had formerly been appointed by the President from a list submitted by the lower house of the territorial legislature. The process of democratization was continued in the following act (March 3, 1811). Any free white male who could produce evidence of having paid a county or territorial tax was enfranchised.[25]

AN ACT to extend the right of suffrage in the Indiana Territory, and for other purposes.

Be it enacted, etc. That each and every free white male person, who shall have attained the age of twenty-one years, and who shall have paid a county or Territorial tax, and who shall have resided one year in said Territory, previous to any general election, and be at the time of any such election a resident of said Territory, shall be entitled to vote for members of the Legislative Council and House of Representatives of the Territorial Legislature, and for a Delegate to the Congress of the United States for said Territory.

Sec. 2. *And be it further enacted,* That the citizens of the Indiana Territory, entitled to vote for Representatives to the General Assembly thereof, may, on the third Monday of April next, and on the third Monday of April biennially thereafter (unless the General Assembly of said Territory shall appoint a different day), elect one Delegate for said Territory to the Congress of the United States, who shall possess the same powers heretofore granted by law to the same.

Sec. 3. *And be it further enacted,* That each and every sheriff that now is or hereafter may be appointed in said Territory, who shall either neglect or refuse to perform the duties required by an act, entitled "An act extending the right of suffrage in the Indiana Territory, and for other purposes," passed in February, one thousand eight hundred and nine, shall be liable to a penalty of one thousand dollars, recoverable by action of debt, in any court of record within

---

[25] *Annals of Congress,* 11 Cong., 3 Sess., 1347-1348; *Laws of the United States,* X, 368-370; Kettleborough (ed.), *Constitution Making in Indiana,* I, 58-59.

the said Territory, one-half for the use of the informer, and the other for the use of the Territory.

Sec. 4. *And be it further enacted,* That any person holding, or who may hereafter hold, any office of profit from the Governor of the Indiana Territory, (justices of the peace and militia officers excepted), shall be ineligible to, and disqualified to act as a member of the Legislative Council or House of Representatives for said Territory.

Sec. 5. *And be it further enacted,* That each and every sheriff, in each and every county, that now is or hereafter may be established in said Territory, shall cause to be held the election prescribed by this act, according to the time and manner prescribed by the laws of said Territory and this act, under the penalty of one thousand dollars, to be recovered in the manner and for the use pointed out by the third section of this act.

Approved, March 3, 1811.

THE STATE CAPITAL ACT, 1813

After Illinois was cut off from Indiana Territory in 1809 Vincennes ceased to be central in relation to the area it served as a capital. Lawrenceburg, Vevay, Madison, Corydon, Salem, and Jeffersonville sought the honor. No action was taken while Harrison was Governor since he preferred Vincennes. In 1813, with John Gibson as acting Governor, the Assembly took up the matter. The House of Representatives favored Madison but the Council would not agree and Corydon was chosen in conference. The act which was dated March 11, 1813, was to be effective by May 1, 1813.[26]

AN ACT *to remove the Seat of Government from the town of Vincennes to the town of Corydon, in the county of Harrison.*

§ 1. BE *it enacted by the Legislative Council and House of Representatives, and it is hereby enacted by the authority of the same,* That from and after the first day of May next, the seat of government of the Indiana territory shall be, and the same is hereby fixed and established in the town of Corydon, in the county of Harrison, and the said seat of government shall be and remain in the said town of Corydon, until altered by law; and it shall be the duty of all officers and all other persons in any way concerned in administering the government of the said territory, and all persons whose duty it is to be at the seat of government of the said territory, or whose functions are or ought to be exercised at the said seat of government, to remove the books, records, papers and proceedings of whatsoever nature or kind they may be, in any wise relating to their offices to the said town of Corydon, in the said county of Harrison, on or before the said first day of May next, and it shall be the duty of all the said officers, and all persons whose duty it is to be and attend at the seat of government to be and attend at the said town of Corydon, in the county of Harrison, from and after the said first day of May next, then and there to attend to, perform, and do whatsoever to their said offices doth belong or in any wise concerned are hereby required to govern themselves accordingly.

§ 2. *And be it further enacted,* That it shall be the duty of the Judges of the General court of the said territory, and they are

---

[26] Louis B. Ewbank and Dorothy L. Riker (eds.), *The Laws of Indiana Territory, 1809-1816 (Indiana Historical Collections,* XX, Indianapolis, 1934), 335-338; Logan Esarey, *A History of Indiana* (2 volumes, Fort Wayne, 1924), I, 239-242.

hereby authorized and required to hold the first term of the said court after the passage of this act at the town of Vincennes, in the county of Knox as heretofore, on the first Tuesday of April next, and the second term of the said General court, after the passage of this act shall be held, and the said Judges are hereby authorised and required to hold the same in the said town of Corydon, in the said county of Harrison, and the said Judges shall continue to hold the said court on the several days which are or may be fixed by law for holding the said courts, and the said town of Corydon, in the said county of Harrison, shall be, and the same is hereby declared to be the place of holding the said General court until altered by law; and all actions, suits, pleas, plaints and causes now depending in the said court, which by the existing laws are required to be tried and decided in the said General court, shall be, and the same are hereby removed from and after the said first day of May next, to the said town of Corydon, in as full, complete and ample a manner as if the said actions, suits, pleas, plaints and causes had been originally brought in the said county of Harrison, and all actions, suits, pleas, plaints and causes had been originally brought in the said county of Harrison; and all actions, suits, pleas, plaints and causes which are now depending in the said court, and which by the existing laws may be tried in the Circuit court, shall be tried in the Circuit court of the county of Knox, which shall be held in the said county, when, and at such times as may or shall be regulated and established by law; and it shall be the duty of the Clerk of the said General court to remove, or cause to be removed all records, books, papers and proceedings of whatsoever kind they may be, in any wise relating to any of the actions, suits, pleas, plaints or causes by this act removed to the said town of Corydon on or before the said first day of May next; and it shall be the further duty of the said Clerk, from and after the said first day of May next, to be and attend at the town of Corydon aforesaid, then and there to do, attend to, and perform whatsoever to his said office may or doth belong, or in any wise appertain.

§ 3. *And be it further enacted,* That if any officer or other person in any wise concerned in administering the government, or the Clerk of the General court, or any other person whose duty it is made by the provisions of this act to remove, or cause to be removed any books, papers, records or other documents or proceedings to the said town of Corydon, or if any person or persons, officer or officers, who are by this act required to be and attend at the said town of Corydon, shall neglect or refuse to do and perform the duties required of them by this act, the person or persons so offending shall each and every of them be fined in a sum not less than one hundred, nor more than twelve hundred dollars, to be recovered by indictment before any court of record for the use of the territory.

§ 4. *And be it further enacted,* That any expense necessarily incurred by any officer in removing the books, papers, records and proceedings pertaining to his said office from Vincennes to the said town of Corydon, agreeably to the requisitions of this act shall be paid out of the territorial treasury; and the governor of this territory is hereby authorized and empowered to order out any number of militia that he may deem necessary for the more safe conveyance of any books, papers, or other thing by this act made necessary to be conveyed to the said town of Corydon.

JAMES DILL,
Speaker of the House of Representatives.

JAs. BEGGS,
President of the Legislative Council.

Approved—March 11, 1813.

JOHN GIBSON.

MEMORIAL FOR STATEHOOD, 1815

Late in 1811 the Territorial Assembly forwarded a petition asking Congress to admit Indiana as an equal member of the Union. The petition was referred to a committee headed by Indiana's delegate, Jonathan Jennings. On March 31, 1812, the committee recommended admission when a territorial census indicated a population of 35,000. Apparently, Congress preferred to adhere to the provision of the Northwest Ordinance prescribing a minimum population of 60,000 for no action was taken. The outbreak of the second war with Britain discouraged further consideration of the matter.[27] The Assembly authorized a census on August 29, 1814, which was submitted to the House of Representatives on January 5, 1816. It showed a population of 63,897.[28] A second petition asking for statehood was approved by the Indiana legislature on December 11, 1815. It noted the results of the census and asked authority to hold a constitutional convention in May, 1816. The memorial asked for seven per cent of the proceeds from the sale of public lands; the grant of one section in each township for the support of common schools; the reservation of three entire townships, one for an academy, a second for a college, and a third for the state capital. Indiana's devotion to "personal freedom" and hostility to "involuntary servitude" was asserted in the concluding paragraph.[29] While virtually all those active in public affairs in Indiana in the territorial period were members of the Democratic-Republican Party of Jefferson and Madison, bitter factional rivalries existed. Politics were highly personal. Harrison and his supporters were opposed by Jennings and his friends. An understanding of the events of the territorial period, including the statehood movement, is facilitated by examining one of the several available analyses of the factional situation.[30]

To the Honorable the Senate and House of Representatives of the United States in Congress Assembled.—

The Memorial of the Legislative Council and the House of Representatives, of the Indiana Territory, Assembled at the town of Corydon, in the Year eighteen hundred and fifteen, in behalf of their constituents, respectfully Sheweth.—

That Whereas the ordinance of congress, for the Government, of this Territory, has

---

[27] *Annals of Congress,* 12 Cong., 1 Sess., 607, 749, 1247; Kettleborough (ed.), *Constitution Making in Indiana,* I, 65-69.

[28] *Ibid.,* I, 68-69.

[29] Ewbank and Riker (eds.), *Laws of Indiana Territory,* 811-814; Vincennes *Western Sun,* January 27, 1816; Kettleborough (ed.), *Constitution Making in Indiana,* I, 69-72.

[30] Dunn, *Indiana,* I, 286-292; Barnhart and Carmony, *Indiana,* I, 143-151.

provided, "That whenever there shall be sixty thousand free inhabitants therein, this Territory shall be admitted into the Union, on an equal footing with the original States." And Whereas by a census taken by the authority of the Legislature of this Territory, it appears from the returns that the number of free white inhabitants, exceeds Sixty thousand, we therefore pray the Honorable Senate and House of Representatives, in congress assembled, to order an election, to be conducted agreeably to the existing laws of this Territory, to be held in the several counties of this Territory, on the first monday of May 1816. for representatives to meet in convention, at the seat of Government of this Territory the   day of   1816. Who when assembled shall determine by a majority of the votes, of all the members elected, Whether it will be expedient or inexpedient, to go into a State Government, and if it be determined expedient, the convention thus assembled, shall have the power to form a constitution and frame of Government, Or if it be deemed inexpedient, to provide for the election of Representatives, to meet in convention, at some future period to form a constitution.—

And Whereas the people of this Territory, have made great sacrifices, by settling on the frontiers, where they have been exposed to dangers and hardships of almost every description, by which means, the lands of the United States, have been greatly increased in value; we feel confident, that congress will be disposed, to grant us seven per cent on all monies received at any of the United States land offices, from the first day of April 1816. for lands already sold, or hereafter to be sold, lying in this Territory, such per centage to be at the disposal of this Government, in such way as may be judged most conducive to the General welfare. It is expected by us that the General Government, will be disposed to confirm to us her grant of township No. 2. South of Range 11. west of the second principal meridian, granted to the Indiana Territory for the use of an Academy, also the reserved Sections 16. in that portion of the Territory where the Indian title has already been extinguished, as well as that which may be hereafter purchased, of the Indians, to be at the disposal of the future State for the use of Schools, and it is further requested and expected, that all coal mines and Salt licks, which may be reserved by the United States, with a sufficiency of land to work them to effect, will be granted to the future State, as well where the Indian title is relinquished as where it is not, as soon as such relinquishment is obtained by the United States. Furthermore as it is conceived by us, that the promotion of useful Knowledge, is the best Guarantee to our civil institutions, and as congress must know something of the difficulties, of raising money in new countries, for the support of universities, we think we do ourselves but justice, in asking a reserve of one entire township, for the support of a college, to be located at some suitable place, on the United States lands in this Territory.—And whereas in the counties of Knox Gibson and Clark, in said Territory, a great quantity, of the lands in said counties, are claimed by private individuals, and confirmed to them by various laws of congress, which lands are so located that those counties will be deprived of the benefits from the sixteenth Section, reserved by the laws of congress, for the use of schools, It is therefore expected, that congress will reserve an equivalent in lands for the use of Schools, in said counties, in proportion to the number of the 16th Section now the property of individuals in said counties.—As it is deemed good policy, that every State should have its Seat of Government as nearly central as the local situation of the country will permit, and as such site proper for the permanent Seat, is not at this time at the disposal of this Territory, or the General Government, it is expected That congress will, Whenever the Indian title shall be extinguished, grant us a township of six miles square, to be selected by such persons, as the future state may appoint; and whereas congress will receive the most correct information from this body, to enable them to proportion the number of representatives to the convention in the different counties, we recommend the following as proportioned to the census of each county, according to their present boundaries to wit.—

Wayne	4.	Washington	5.
Franklin	5.	Harrison	4.
Dearborn	3.	Knox	5.
Switzerland	1.	Gibson	4.
Jefferson	3.	Posey	1.
Clark	5.	Warrick. &,	
Perry	1.		

And whereas the inhabitants of this Territory, are principally composed of emigrants, from every part of the union, and as various in their customs and sentiments, as in their persons, we think it prudent at this time to express to the General Government, our attachment to the fundamental principles of Legislation, prescribed by congress in their ordinance for the Government of this Territory, particularly as respects personal freedom and involuntary servitude, and hope that they may be continued as the basis of our constitution.—

DENNIS PENNINGTON *Speaker of the House of representatives*

DAVID ROBB *president of the Legislative Council—*

THE ENABLING ACT, 1816

The Indiana statehood petition was referred to select committees in both houses of Congress. On January 5, 1816, the House Committee of which Jennings was chairman reported favorably and submitted a bill for an Enabling Act. The bill passed the House on March 30 by a vote of 108 to 3. It was approved in the Senate on April 13 and signed by President Madison on April 19. Mississippi Territory was also seeking admission over some anti-slavery opposition at this time. The close relation between the passage of the two enabling acts suggests that this is the beginning of the "twin state" process, that is, the admission of a slave state and a free state simultaneously. The demands of the territorial Assembly were not fully met but Congress did not deal with Indiana ungenerously. The Enabling Act provided for the election of delegates to the constitutional convention on May 13. The convention was to meet on June 10. This permitted a campaign of approximately ten days.[31]

An act to enable the people of the Indiana Territory to form a constitution and state government, and for the admission of such state into the Union on an equal footing with the original states.

Be it enacted by the senate and house of representatives of the United States of America, in congress assembled, That the inhabitants of the territory of Indiana be, and they are hereby authorized to form for themselves a constitution and state government, and to assume such name as they shall deem proper; and the said state, when formed, shall be admitted into the union upon the same footing with the original states, in all respects whatever.

Sec. 2. *And be it further enacted,* That the said state shall consist of all the territory included within the following boundaries, to wit: bounded on the east, by the meridian line which forms the western boundary of the state of Ohio; on the south, by the river Ohio, from the mouth of the Great Miami river, to the mouth of the river Wabash; on the west, by a line drawn along the middle of the Wabash from its mouth, to a point, where a due north line drawn from the town of Vincennes, would last touch the north western shore of the said river; and from thence by a due north line, until the same shall intersect an east and west line, drawn through a point ten miles north

[31] *Acts Passed at the First Session of the Fourteenth Congress of the United States,* 59-61; *U. S. Statutes at Large,* III, 289-291; Kettleborough (ed.), *Constitution Making in Indiana,* I, 73-77; Carter (ed.), *Territorial Papers,* VIII, 404-408.

of the southern extreme of lake Michigan; on the north, by the said east and west line, until the same shall intersect the first mentioned meridian line which forms the western boundary of the state of Ohio: *Provided,* That the convention hereinafter provided for, when formed, shall ratify the boundaries aforesaid; otherwise they shall be and remain as now prescribed by the ordinance for the government of the territory northwest of the river Ohio: *Provided also,* That the said state shall have concurrent jurisdiction on the river Wabash, with the state to be formed west thereof, so far as the said river shall form a common boundary to both.

Sec. 3. *And be it further enacted,* That all male citizens of the United States, who shall have arrived at the age of twenty one years, and resided within the said territory, at least one year previous to the day of election, and shall have paid a county or territorial tax; and all persons having in other respects the legal qualifications to vote for representatives in the general assembly of the said territory be, and they are hereby authorized to choose representatives to form a convention, who shall be apportioned amongst the several counties within the said territory, according to the apportionment made by the legislature thereof, at their last session, to wit: from the county of Wayne, four representatives; from the county of Franklin, five representatives; from the county of Dearborn, three representatives; from the county of Switzerland, one representative; from the county of Jefferson, three representatives; from the county of Clark, five representatives; from the county of Harrison, five representatives; from the county of Washington, five representatives; from the county of Knox, five representatives; from the county of Gibson, four representatives; from the county of Posey, one representative; from the county of Warrick, one representative; and from the county of Perry, one representative. And the election for the representatives aforesaid, shall be holden on the second Monday of May, one thousand eight hundred and sixteen, throughout the several counties in the said territory; and shall be conducted in the same manner, and under the same penalties, as prescribed by the laws of said territory, regulating elections therein for members of the house of representatives.

Sec. 4. *And be it further enacted,* That the members of the convention, thus duly elected be, and they are hereby authorized to meet at the seat of the government of the said territory, on the second

Monday of June next, which convention, when met, shall first determine, by a majority of the whole number elected, whether it be, or be not expedient, at that time, to form a constitution and state government, for the people within the said territory, and if it be determined to be expedient, the convention shall be, and hereby are authorized, to form a constitution and state government: or if it be deemed more expedient, the said convention shall provide by ordinance for electing representatives to form a constitution, or frame of government; which said representatives shall be chosen in such manner, and in such proportion, and shall meet at such time and place, as shall be prescribed by the said ordinance, and shall then form, for the people of said territory, a constitution and state government: *Provided,* That the same, whenever formed, shall be republican, and not repugnant to those articles of the ordinance of the thirteenth of July, one thousand seven hundred and eighty-seven, which are declared to be irrevocable between the original states, and the people and states of the territory northwest of the river Ohio; excepting so much of said articles as relate to the boundaries of the states therein to be formed.

Sec. 5. *And be it further enacted,* That until the next general census shall be taken, the said state shall be entitled to one representative in the house of representatives of the United States.

Sec. 6. *And be it further enacted,* That the following propositions be, and the same are hereby offered to the convention of the said territory of Indiana, when formed, for their free acceptance or rejection, which, if accepted by the convention, shall be obligatory upon the United States.

First. That the section numbered sixteen, in every township, and when such section has been sold, granted or disposed of, other lands, equivalent thereto, and most contiguous to the same, shall be granted to the inhabitants of such township for the use of schools.

Second. That all salt springs within the said territory, and the land reserved for the use of the same, together with such other lands as may, by the president of the United States, be deemed necessary and proper for working the said salt springs, not exceeding, in the whole, the quantity contained in thirty-six entire sections shall be granted to the said state, for the use of the people of the said state, the same to be used under such terms, conditions, and regulations as the legislature of the said state shall direct: provided the said legislature shall never sell nor lease the same, for a longer period than ten years at any one time.

Third. That five per cent of the net proceeds of the lands lying within the said territory, and which shall be sold by Congress from and after the first day of December next, after deducting all expenses incident to the same, shall be reserved for making public roads and canals, of which three-fifths shall be applied to those objects within the said state, under the direction of the legislature thereof, and two-fifths to the making of a road or roads leading to the said state under the direction of Congress.

Fourth. That one entire township, which shall be designated by the president of the United States, in addition to the one heretofore reserved for that purpose, shall be reserved for the use of a seminary of learning, and vested in the legislature of the said state, to be appropriated solely to the use of such seminary by the said legislature.

Fifth. That four sections of land be, and the same are hereby granted to the said state, for the purpose of fixing their seat of government thereon, which four sections shall, under the direction of the legislature of said state, be located at any time, in such township and range, as the legislature aforesaid may select, on such lands as may hereafter be acquired by the United States, from the Indian tribes within the said territory: *Provided,* That such locations shall be made prior to the public sale of the lands of the United States, surrounding such location: *And provided always,* That the five foregoing propositions, herein offered, are, on the conditions that the convention of the said state shall provide by an ordinance irrevocable, without the consent of the United States, that every and each tract of land sold by the United States, from and after the first day of December next, shall be and remain exempt from any tax, laid by order or under any authority of the state, whether for state, county or township, or any other purpose whatever, for the term of five years, from and after the day of sale.

[*Approved, April 19, 1816*]

LETTER FROM THE CONGRESSIONAL DELEGATE

A letter from Jennings dated April 16 reporting the action of Congress was printed in the *Western Sun* on May 11. The *Sun* had learned of the passage of the Enabling Act on May 2. Voting places in Knox County were announced in the issue of May 4.[32]

Washington City, April 16th, 1816.

. . . . The act to enable the people of Indiana to form a constitution and State government has passed both Houses of Congress, and will undoubtedly receive the President's signature. The act fixes the second Monday of May next, for the election of members of the convention in the several counties. Each county has the number of members to elect, as were allotted to each by the Territorial legislature except the county of Harrison. Every citizen qualified to vote for members of the Territorial legislature is qualified to vote for members of the convention, and the second Monday of June next is fixed by the act for the meeting of the convention when elected at the seat of Government. The times fixed for the election and meeting of the convention, are as well suited to every interest and circumstance connected with the proposed important change of our form of government as I was enabled to select when every consideration was duly weighed, and I trust will be so considered when the convention shall act officially on the subject. With regard to the grants and conditions contained in this act, the convention when met will be able to form a correct estimate. Allow me, however, to state that they are at least as advantageous if not more so, than those granted to any other Territory on similar occasions. . . .

Very respectfully,
I am very obediently yours,
JONATHAN JENNINGS.

---

[32] *Western Sun*, May 11, May 4, 1816.

KNOX COUNTY CONVENTION ELECTION, 1816

On Monday the 13th inst. an election will be held in the different townships in this county, at the following places for five persons to represent this county in the convention to form a constitution—in Vincennes township, at the court house; in Decker township, at the house of Adam Harness; in Harrison township, at the house of George Leech; in Palmyra township, at the house of William Purcell; in Busseron township, at the house of Joseph Latshaw; in Widner township, at the house of John Widner; in Hawkins township, at Liverpool; and in Perry township, at the house of Samuel Perry.

B. V. Beckes, S. K. C.

May 2, 1816.

INDIANA'S FIRST CONSTITUTION, 1816

On June 10, 1816, the constitutional delegates assembled at Corydon. As a group they were men of high quality. Of the forty-three elected twenty-six had southern antecedents but they had come from the democratic backcountry rather than the plantation tidewater. Eleven were from northern states and six were foreign-born. Jonathan Jennings was chosen as president and William Hendricks as secretary of the convention. By a vote of 33 to 8 they asserted that it was expedient to form a constitution. In preparing Indiana's fundamental law they borrowed heavily from existing state constitutions especially those of Virginia, Ohio, and Kentucky. They produced a strongly democratic document for that period which served Indiana well for thirty-five years. Slavery was forbidden and an advanced concept of state responsibility for public education was incorporated. The amending process was to prove cumbersome. The new constitution went into effect without submission to the people.[33]

PREAMBLE

We the Representatives of the people of the Territory of Indiana, in Convention met, at Corydon, on monday the tenth day of June in the year of our Lord eighteen hundred and sixteen, and of the Independence of the United States, the fortieth, having the right of admission into the General Government, as a member of the union, consistent with the constitution of the United States, the ordinance of Congress of one thousand seven hundred and eighty seven, and the law of Congress, entitled "An act to enable the people of the Indiana Territory to form a Constitution and State Government, and for the admission of such state into the union, on an equal footing with the original States" in order to establish Justice, promote the welfare, and secure the blessings of liberty to ourselves and our posterity; do ordain and establish the following constitution or form of Government, and do mutually agree with each other to form ourselves into a free and Independent state, by the name of the State of Indiana.

ARTICLE I.

Sect. 1st. That the general, great and essential principles of liberty and free Government may be recognized and unalterably

---

[33] Manuscript constitution, Indiana State Library; Kettleborough (ed.), *Constitution Making in Indiana,* I, 83-125; Barnhart and Carmony, *Indiana,* I, 151-160; Dunn, *Indiana,* I, 295-313.

established; WE declare, That all men are born equally free and independent, and have certain natural, inherent, and unalienable rights; among which are the enjoying and defending life and liberty, and of acquiring, possessing, and protecting property, and pursuing and obtaining happiness and safety.

Sect. 2.   That all power is inherent in the people; and all free Governments are founded on their authority, and instituted for their peace, safety and happiness. For the advancement of these ends, they have at all times an unalienable and indefeasible right to alter or reform their Government in such manner as they may think proper.

Sect. 3.   That all men have a natural and indefeasible right to worship Almighty God, according to the dictates of their own consciences: That no man shall be compelled to attend, erect, or support any place of Worship, or to maintain any ministry against his consent: That no human authority can, in any case whatever, control or interfere with the rights of conscience: And that no preference shall ever be given by law to any religious societies, or modes of worship; and no religious test shall be required as a qualification to any office of trust or profit.

Sect. 4.   That elections shall be free and equal.

Sect. 5.   That in all civil cases, when the value in controversy shall exceed the sum of twenty dollars, and in all criminal cases, except in petit misdemeanors which shall be punished by fine only, not exceeding three dollars, in such manner as the Legislature may prescribe by law; the right of trial by Jury shall remain inviolate.

Sect. 6th.   That no power of suspending the operation of the laws, shall be exercised, except by the Legislature, or its authority.

Sect. 7th.   That no man's particular services shall be demanded, or property taken, or applied to public use, without the consent of his representatives or without a just compensation being made therefor.

Sect. 8.   The rights of the people, to be secure in their persons, houses, papers, and effects, against unreasonable searches, and seizures, shall not be violated: and no warrant shall issue, but upon probable cause, supported by oath, or affirmation, and particularly describing the place to be searched, and the persons or things to be seized.

Sect. 9th.   That the printing presses shall be free to every person, who undertakes to examine the proceedings of the Legislature, or any branch of Government; and no law shall ever be made to restrain the right thereof. The free communication of thoughts, and opinions, is one of the invaluable rights of man; and every Citizen may freely speak, write, and print on any subject, being responsible for the abuse of that liberty.

Sect. 10. In prosecutions for the publication of papers investigating the official conduct of officers, or men in a public capacity, or when the matter published is proper for the public information, the truth thereof may be given in evidence; and in all indictments for libels, the Jury shall have a right to determine the law and the facts, under the direction of the court, as in other cases.

Sect. 11. That all Courts shall be open, and every person, for an injury done him, in his lands, goods, person, or reputation shall have remedy by the due course of law; and right and justice administered without denial or delay.

Sect. 12. That no person arrested, or confined in Jail, shall be treated with unnecessary rigour, or be put to answer any criminal charge, but by presentment Indictment, or impeachment.

Sect. 13. That in all criminal prosecutions, the accused hath a right to be heard by himself and counsel, to demand the nature and cause of the accusation against him, and to have a copy thereof; to meet the witnesses face to face, to have compulsory process for obtaining witnesses in his favour, and in prosecutions by indictment, or presentment, a speedy public trial by an impartial Jury of the County or district in which the offence shall have been committed; and shall not be compelled to give evidence against himself, nor shall be twice put in jeopardy for the same offence.

Sect. 14. That all persons shall be bailable by sufficient sureties, unless for capital offences, when the proof is evident, or the presumption great; and the privilege of the writ of habeas corpus shall not be suspended, unless, in case of rebellion or invasion, the public safety may require it.

Sect. 15. Excessive bail shall not be required, excessive fines shall not be imposed, nor cruel and unusual punishments inflicted.

Sect. 16. All penalties shall be proportioned to the nature of the offence.

Sect. 17.   The person of a debtor, where there is not strong presumption of fraud, shall not be continued in prison, after delivering up his estate, for the benefit of his creditor, or creditors, in such manner as shall be prescribed by law.

Sect. 18.   No ex post facto law, nor any law impairing the validity of contracts, shall ever be made, and no conviction shall work corruption of blood, nor forfeiture of estate.

Sect. 19.   That the people have a right to assemble together in a peaceable manner, to consult for their common good, to instruct their representatives, and to apply to the Legislature for redress of grievances.

Sect. 20.   That the people have a right to bear arms for the defence of themselves, and the state; and that the military shall be kept in strict subordination to the civil power.

Sect. 21.   That no soldier shall, in time of peace, be quartered in any house without the consent of the owner, nor in time of war, but in a manner to be prescribed by law.

Sect. 22.   That the Legislature shall not grant any title of nobility, or hereditary distinctions, nor create any office, the appointment to which, shall be for a longer term than good behaviour.

Sect. 23.   That emigration from the state shall not be prohibited.

Sect. 24.   To guard against any encroachments on the rights herein retained, we declare, that every thing in this article, is excepted out of the general powers of Government, and shall forever remain inviolable.

ARTICLE II.

The powers of the Government of Indiana shall be divided into three distinct departments, and each of them be confided to a separate body of Magistracy, to wit: those which are Legislative to one, those which are Executive to another, and those which are Judiciary to another: And no person or collection of persons, being of one of those departments, shall exercise any power properly attached to either of the others, except in the instances herein expressly permitted.

ARTICLE III.

Sect. 1.   The Legislative authority of this state, shall be vested in a general assembly, which shall consist of a Senate, and house of Representatives, both to be elected by the people.

Sect. 2.   The General Assembly may, within two years after their first meeting, and shall, in the year eighteen hundred and twenty, and every subsequent term of five years, cause an enumeration to be made, of all the white male inhabitants above the age of twenty-one years.   The number of Representatives shall, at the several periods of making such enumeration, be fixed by the General Assembly, and apportioned among the several counties, according to the number of white male inhabitants, above twenty-one years of age in each; and shall never be less than twenty-five, nor greater than thirty-six, until the number of white male inhabitants above twenty-one years of age, shall be twenty-two thousand; and after that event, at such ratio, that the whole number of Representatives shall never be less than thirty-six, nor exceed one hundred.

Sect. 3.   The Representatives shall be chosen annually, by the qualified electors of each County respectively, on the first Monday of August.

Sect. 4.   No person shall be a Representative, unless he shall have attained the age of twenty-one years, and shall be a Citizen of the united States, and an inhabitant of this state, and shall also have resided within the limits of the County, in which he shall be chosen, one year next preceeding his election; if the County shall have been so long erected, but if not, then within the limits of the County or Counties out of which it shall have been taken; unless he shall have been absent on the public business of the united States, or of this state, and shall have paid a State or County tax.

Sect. 5.   The Senators shall be chosen for three years, on the first Monday in August, by the qualified voters for Representatives; and on their being convened, in consequence of the first election, they shall be divided by lot, from their respective Counties, or districts, as near as can be, into three classes; the seats of the senators of the first class shall be vacated at the expiration of the first year; & the second class, at the expiration of the second year; and of the third class, at the expiration of the third year; so that one third thereof, as near as possible, may be annually chosen forever thereafter.

Sect. 6. The number of senators shall, at the several periods of making the enumeration before mentioned, be fixed by the General Assembly, and apportioned among the several Counties or districts, to be established by law, according to the number of white male inhabitants of the age of twenty-one years in each, and shall never be less than one third, nor more than one half of the number of Representatives.

Sect. 7. No person shall be a senator, unless he shall have attained the age of twenty-five years, and shall be a Citizen of the united States, and shall, next preceeding the election, have resided two years in the state, the last twelve months of which, in the County or district in which he may be elected; if the county or district shall have been so long erected, but if not, then within the limits of the County, or Counties, district or districts, out of which the same shall have been taken; unless he shall have been absent on the public business of the united States, or of this state, and shall moreover, have paid a State or County tax.

Sect. 8. The house of Representatives, when assembled, shall choose a Speaker, and its other officers, and the Senate shall choose its officers, except the president; and each shall be judges of the qualifications and elections of its members; and sit upon its own adjournments. Two thirds of each house shall constitute a quorum to do business, but a smaller number may adjourn from day to day, and compel the attendance of absent members.

Sect. 9. Each house shall keep a Journal of its proceedings, and publish them: The yeas and nays of the members, on any question, shall, at the request of any two of them. be entered on the Journals.

Sect. 10. Any one member of either house, shall have liberty to dissent from, and protest against any act or resolution, which he may think injurious to the public, or any individual or individuals, and have the reason of his dissent entered on the Journals.

Sect. 11. Each house may determine the rules of its proceedings, punish its members for disorderly behaviour, and, with the concurrence of two-thirds, expel a member, but not a second time for the same cause; and shall have all other powers necessary for a branch of the Legislature of a free and independent State.

Sect. 12. When vacancies happen in either branch of the General Assembly, the Governor, or the person exercising the power of Governor, shall issue writs of election to fill such vacancies.

Sect. 13. Senators and Representatives shall, in all cases except treason, felony, or breach of the peace, be privileged from arrest, during the Session of the General Assembly, and in going to, or returning from the same; and for any Speech or debate in either house, they shall not be questioned in any other place.

Sect. 14. Each house may punish, by imprisonment, during their Session, any person, not a member, who shall be guilty of any disrespect to the house, by any disorderly, or contemptuous behaviour in their presence; provided such imprisonment shall not, at any one time, exceed twenty-four hours.

Sect. 15. The doors of each house, and of committees of the whole, shall be kept open, except in such cases as, in the opinion of the House, may require secrecy. Neither house shall, without the consent of the other, adjourn for more than two days, nor to any other place than that in which the two houses shall be sitting.

Sect. 16. Bills may originate in either house, but may be altered, amended or rejected by the other.

Sect. 17. Every bill shall be read on three different days in each house, unless, in case of urgency, two-thirds of the house, when such bill may be depending, shall deem it expedient to dispense with this rule: And every bill having passed both houses, shall be signed by the president and speaker of their respective houses.

Sect. 18. The style of the laws of this State shall be, "Be it enacted by the General assembly of the State of Indiana."

Sect. 19. All bills for raising revenue shall originate in the house of Representatives, but the senate may amend or reject, as in other bills.

Sect. 20. No person, holding any office under the authority of the President of the United States, or of this State, Militia officers excepted, shall be eligible to a seat in either branch of the General Assembly; unless he resign his office, previous to his election; nor shall any member of either branch of the General Assembly, during the time for which he is elected, be eligible to any office, the appointment of which is vested in the General Assembly: Provided That nothing, in this constitution, shall be so construed, as to prevent any member of the first Session of the first General Assembly from accepting any office, that is created by this constitution, or the Constitution of the united States, and the salaries of which are established.

Sect. 21. No money shall be drawn from the Treasury but in consequence of appropriations made by law.

Sect. 22. An accurate Statement of the receipts and expenditures of the public money shall be attached to, and published with the laws, at every annual session of the General Assembly.

Sect. 23. The house of Representatives shall have the sole power of impeaching; but a majority of all the members elected must concur in such impeachment. All impeachments shall be tried by the senate, and when sitting for that purpose, the senators shall be upon oath or affirmation to do justice according to law and evidence. No person shall be convicted without the concurrence of a majority of all the senators elected.

Sect. 24. The Governor, and all civil officers of the State, shall be removed from office, on impeachment for, and conviction of treason, bribery, or other high crimes and misdemeanors; but Judgment in such cases, shall not extend further than removal from office, and disqualification to hold any office of honour, profit, or trust, under this State. The party, whether convicted or acquitted shall, nevertheless, be liable to indictment trial, judgment, and punishment, according to law.

Sect. 25. The first session of the General Assembly shall commence on the first Monday of November next, and forever after, the General Assembly shall meet on the first Monday in December, in every year, and at no other period, unless directed by law, or provided for by this Constitution.

Sect. 26. No person, who hereafter may be a collector, or holder of public money, shall have a seat in either house of the General Assembly, until such person shall have accounted for, and paid into the Treasury all sums for which he may be accountable.

ARTICLE IV.

Sect. 1st. The Supreme Executive power of this State shall be vested in a Governor, who shall be styled, the Governor of the State of Indiana.

Sect. 2. The Governor shall be chosen by the qualified electors, on the first monday in August, at the places where they shall respectively vote for Representatives. The returns of every election for Governor shall be sealed up and transmitted to the seat of Government, directed to the speaker of the house of Representatives, who shall open and publish them in the presence of both houses of the General assembly. The person having the highest number of votes shall be governor, but if two or more shall be equal, and highest in votes, one of them shall be chosen Governor by the joint vote of the members of both houses. Contested elections shall be determined by a committee, to be selected from both houses of the General assembly and formed and regulated in such manner as shall be directed by law.

Sect. 3. The Governor shall hold his office during three years, from and after the third day of the first session of the General assembly, next ensuing his election, and until a successor shall be chosen and qualified, and shall not be capable of holding it longer than six years in any term of nine years.

Sect. 4. He shall be at least thirty years of age, and shall have been a citizen of the united States ten years, and have resided in the State five years next preceeding his Election; unless he shall have been absent on the business of the State, or of the United States; provided that this shall not disqualify any person from the office of Governor, who shall be a citizen of the United States, and Shall have resided in the Indiana Territory two years next preceeding the adoption of this Constitution.

Sect. 5. No member of Congress, or person holding any office under the united States, or this State, shall exercise the office of Governor, or Lieutenant Governor.

Sect. 6. The Governor shall, at Stated times, receive for his services a compensation, which shall neither be increased nor diminished during the term for which he shall have been elected.

Sect. 7. He shall be commander in chief of the army and Navy of this State and of the Militia thereof, except when they shall be called into service of the United States, but he shall not command personally in the field unless he shall be advised so to do by a resolution of the General assembly.

Sect. 8. He shall nominate, and, by and with the advice and consent of the senate, appoint and commission all officers, the appointment of which is not otherwise directed by this Constitution, and all offices which may be created by the General Assembly, shall be filled in such manner as may be directed by law.

Sect. 9. Vacancies that may happen in offices, the appointment of which is vested in the Governor, and senate, or in the General Assembly, shall be filled by the Governor, during the recess of the General Assembly, by granting Commissions that shall expire at the end of the next Session.

Sect. 10. He shall have power to remit fines and forfeitures, grant reprieves and pardons, except in cases of impeachments.

Sect. 11. He may require information in writing, from the officers in the executive department, upon any subject relating to the duties of their respective offices.

Sect. 12. He shall, from time to time, give to the General Assembly information of the affairs of the State, and recommend to their consideration, such measures as he shall deem expedient.

Sect. 13. He may, in extraordinary occasions, convene the General Assembly at the seat of Government, or at a different place, if that shall have become, since their last adjournment, dangerous from an enemy, or from contagious disorders, and in case of a disagreement between the two houses with respect to the time of adjournment, adjourn them to such time as he shall think proper, not beyond the time of their next annual Session.

Sect. 14. He shall take care that the laws be faithfully executed.

Sect. 15. A Lieutenant Governor shall be chosen at every election for a Governor, in the same manner, continue in office for the same time, and possess the same qualifications. In voting for Governor, and Lieutenant Governor, the electors shall distinguish whom they vote for as Governor, and whom, as Lieutenant Governor.

Sect. 16. He shall, by virtue of his office, be President of the Senate, have a right, when in Committee of the whole, to debate and vote on all subjects, and when the senate are equally divided, to give the casting vote.

Sect. 17.   In case of impeachment of the Governor, his removal from office, death, refusal to qualify, resignation, or absence from the State, the Lieutenant Governor shall exercise all the powers and authority appertaining to the office of Governor, until another be duly qualified, or the Governor absent, or impeached, shall return, or be acquitted.

Sect. 18.   Whenever the Government shall be administered by the Lieutenant Governor, or he shall be unable to attend as President of the senate, the senate shall elect one of their own members as president for that occasion.   And if during the vacancy of the office of Governor, the Lieutenant Governor shall be impeached, removed from office, refuse to qualify, resign, die, or be absent from the State, the President of the senate pro tem, shall in like manner administer the Government, until he shall be superseded by a Governor or Lieutenant Governor.   The Lieutenant Governor, while he acts as president of the senate, shall receive, for his services the same Compensation which shall, for the same period, be allowed to the Speaker of the house of Representatives and no more: and during the time he administers the Government as Governor, shall receive the same compensation which the governor would have received, and been entitled to, had he been employed in the duties of his office, and no more.

Sect. 19.   The President *pro tempore* of the senate, during the time he administers the Government, shall receive in like manner, the same compensation, which the Governor would have received, had he been employed in the duties of his office, and no more.

Sect. 20.   If the Lieutenant Governor shall be called upon to administer the Government, and shall, while in such administration, resign, die, or be absent from the State, during the recess of the General Assembly, it shall be the duty of the Secretary of State, for the time being, to convene the Senate for the purpose of choosing a president *pro tempore*.

Sect. 21.   A secretary of state shall be chosen by the joint ballot of both houses of the General Assembly, and be commissioned by the Governor for four years, or until a new secretary be chosen and qualified.   He shall keep a fair register, and attest all the official acts and proceedings of the Governor, and shall, when required, lay the same and all papers, minutes and vouchers, relative thereto, before either house of the General assembly, and shall perform such other duties as may be enjoined him by law.

Sect. 22. Every bill, which shall have passed both houses of the General assembly, shall be presented to the Governor: if he approve, he shall sign it; but if not, he shall return it with his objections, to the house in which it have originated, who shall enter the objections at large upon their Journals and proceed to reconsider it; if after such reconsideration, a majority of all the members elected to that house shall agree to pass the bill, it shall be sent, with the objections, to the other house, by which it shall likewise be reconsidered, and if approved by a majority of all the members elected to that house, it shall be a law; but, in such cases the votes of both houses shall be determined by yeas and nays, and the names of the persons voting for, and against the bill, shall be entered on the Journals of each house respectively. If any bill shall not be returned by the Governor within five days (Sundays excepted) after it shall have been presented to him, it shall be a law, in like manner as if he had signed it: unless the General adjournment prevents its return, in which case it shall be a law, unless sent back within three days after their next meeting.

Sect. 23. Every resolution, to which the concurrence of both houses may be necessary, shall be presented to the Governor, and before it shall take effect, be approved by him, or being disapproved, shall be repassed by a majority of all the members elected to both houses, according to the rules and limitations prescribed in case of a bill.

Sect. 24. There shall be elected, by joint ballot of both houses of the General Assembly, a Treasurer, and Auditor, whose powers and duties shall be prescribed by law, and who shall hold their offices three years, and until their successors be appointed and qualified.

Sect. 25. There shall be elected in each County, by the qualified electors thereof, one Sheriff, and one Coroner, at the times and places of holding elections for members of the General assembly. They shall continue in office two years, and until successors shall be chosen and duly qualified: provided, that no person shall be eligible to the office of sheriff more than four years in any term of six years.

Sect. 26. There shall be a seal of this State, which shall be kept by the Governor and used by him officially, and shall be called, the seal of the State of Indiana.

ARTICLE V.

Sect. 1st. The Judiciary power of this State, both as to matters of law and equity, shall be vested in one Supreme Court, in Circuit Courts, and in such other inferior Courts, as the General Assembly may from time to time, direct and establish.

Sect. 2nd. The Supreme Court shall consist of three Judges, any two of whom shall form a quorum, and shall have appellate Jurisdiction only which shall be co-extensive with the limits of the State, under such restrictions, and regulations, not repugnant to this constitution, as may from time to time be prescribed by law. Provided nothing in this article shall be so construed, as to prevent the General Assembly from giving the Supreme Court original Jurisdiction in Capital cases, and cases in chancery, where the President of the Circuit Court, may be interested or prejudiced.

Sect. 3rd. The Circuit Courts shall each consist of a President, and two associate Judges. The State shall be divided by law into three circuits, for each of which, a president shall be appointed, who during his continuance in office, shall reside therein. The President and associate Judges, in their respective Counties, shall have Common law and chancery Jurisdiction, as also complete criminal Jurisdiction, in all such cases and in such manner, as may be prescribed by law. The President alone, in the absence of the associate Judges, or the President and one of the associate Judges, in the absence of the other shall be competent to hold a Court, as also the two associate Judges, in the absence of the President, shall be competent to hold a Court, except in capital cases, and cases in chancery, provided, that nothing herein contained, shall prevent the General Assembly from increasing the number of circuits, and Presidents, as the exigencies of the State may from time to time require.

Sect. 4. The Judges of the supreme Court, the Circuit, and other inferior Courts, shall hold their offices during the term of seven years, if they shall so long behave well, and shall at stated times receive for their services, a compensation which shall not be diminished, during their continuance in office.

Sect. 5. The Judges of the Supreme Court shall by virtue of their offices, be conservators of the peace throughout the State, as also the Presidents of the Circuit Courts, in their respective Circuits, and the associate Judges in their respective Counties.

Sect. 6. The Supreme Court shall hold its sessions at the seat of Government, at such times as shall be prescribed by law: And the circuit Courts shall be held in the respective Counties as may be directed by law.

Sect. 7. The Judges of the supreme Court shall be appointed by the Governor, by and with the advice, and consent of the senate. The Presidents of the circuit Courts shall be appointed by Joint Ballot of both branches of the General Assembly, and the associate Judges of the Circuit Courts, shall be elected by the qualified electors in the respective Counties.

Sect. 8. The supreme Court shall appoint its own Clerk, and the clerks of the circuit Court, in the several Counties, shall be elected by the qualified electors, in the several Counties, but no person shall be eligible to the office of clerk of the Circuit Court in any County, unless he shall first have obtained, from one or more of the Judges of the Supreme Court, or from one or more of the Presidents of the Circuit Courts, a certificate that he is qualified to execute the duties of the office of Clerk of the circuit Court; provided that nothing herein Contained shall prevent the circuit Courts in each County, from appointing a clerk pro tem, until a qualified Clerk may be duly elected, and provided also, that the said clerks respectively when qualified, and elected, shall hold their offices seven years, and no longer, unless re-appointed.

Sect. 9. All clerks shall be removable by impeachment as in other cases.

Sect. 10. When any vacancies happen in any of the Courts occasioned by the death, resignation, or removal from office of any Judge of the supreme, or Circuit Courts, or any of the clerks of the said Courts, a successor shall be appointed in the same manner, as herein before prescribed, who shall hold his office for the period which his predecessor had to serve, and no longer unless re-appointed.

Sect. 11. The style of all process shall be "The State of Indiana." All prosecutions shall be carried on in the name and by the authority of the State of Indiana; and all indictments shall conclude, against the peace and dignity of the same.

Sect. 12. A competent number of Justices of the peace shall be elected by the qualified electors in each Township, in the several Counties, and shall continue in office five years, if they shall so long behave well, whose powers, and duties shall, from time to time, be regulated and defined by law.

ARTICLE VI.

Sect. 1st. In all elections, not otherwise provided for by this constitution, every white male Citizen of the united States, of the age of twenty-one years and upwards, who has resided in the State, one year immediately preceeding such election, shall be entitled to vote in the County where he resides; except such as shall be enlisted in the army of the united States or their allies.

Sect. 2. All elections shall be by ballot; provided that the General Assembly may, if they deem it more expedient at their Session in eighteen hundred and twenty-one, change the mode so as to vote *viva voce,* after which time it shall remain unalterable.

Sect. 3. Electors shall in all cases, except treason felony, or breach of the peace, be free from arrest, in going to, during their attendance at, and in returning home from elections.

Sect. 4. The General Assembly shall have full power to exclude from electing, or being elected, any person convicted of any infamous crime.

Sect. 5. Nothing in this article shall be so construed as to prevent citizens of the united States, who were actual residents at the time of adopting this constitution, and who, by the existing laws of this Territory are entitled to vote or persons who have been absent from home on a visit, or necessary business, from the privilege of electors.

ARTICLE VII.

Sect. 1st. The Militia of the State of Indiana shall consist of all free able bodied male persons; Negroes, Mulattoes and Indians excepted, resident in the said state, between the ages of eighteen, and forty-five years, except such persons as now are, or hereafter may be exempted by the laws of the United States, or of this State; and shall be armed, equipped, and trained, as the general Assembly may provide by law.

Sect. 2.   No person or persons conscientiously scrupulous of bearing arms, shall be compelled to do Militia duty; provided such person or persons shall pay an equivalent for such exemption; which equivalent shall be collected annually, by a civil officer, and be hereafter fixed by law, and shall be equal as near as may be, to the lowest fines assessed on those privates in the Militia, who may neglect or refuse to perform Militia duty.

Sect. 3.   Captains and subalterns shall be elected by those persons in their respective Company districts, who are subject to perform Militia duty, and the captain of each Company shall appoint the non-commissioned officers to said company.

Sect. 4.   Majors shall be elected by those persons within the bounds of their respective Battalion districts, subject to perform Militia duty, and Colonels shall be elected by those persons within the bounds of their respective Regimental districts, subject to perform Militia duty.

Sect. 5.   Brigadier Generals shall be elected by the commissioned officers within the bounds of their respective brigades, and Major Generals shall be elected by the Commissioned officers within the bounds of their respective Divisions.

Sect. 6.   Troops and squadrons of Cavalry, and companies of Artillery riflemen, grenadiers, or light infantry, may be formed in the said state, in such manner as shall be prescribed by law: provided, however, that every troop or squadron of Cavalry, company of Artillery, riflemen, grenadiers, or light infantry which may hereafter be formed within the said state, shall elect their own officers.

Sect. 7.   The Governor shall appoint the adjutant general, and quarter-master generals, as also his aids de camp.

Sect. 8.   Major Generals shall appoint their aids de camp, and all other Division Staff officers; Brigadier Generals shall appoint their Brigade Majors, and all other Brigade Staff officers; and Colonels shall appoint their Regimental Staff officers.

Sect. 9.   All militia officers shall be commissioned by the Governor, and shall hold their Commissions during good behaviour, or until they arrive at the age of sixty years.

Sect. 10.   The General Assembly shall, by law, fix the method of dividing the militia of the said State, into Divisions, Brigades, Regiments, Battalions, and Companies, and shall also fix the rank of all staff officers.

ARTICLE VIII.

Sect. 1.   Every twelfth year, after this constitution shall have taken effect, at the general election held for Governor there shall be a poll opened, in which the qualified Electors of the State shall express, by vote, whether they are in favour of calling a convention, or not, and if there should be a majority of all the votes given at such election, in favour of a convention, the Governor shall inform the next General Assembly thereof, whose duty it shall be to provide, by law, for the election of the members to the convention, the number thereof, and the time and place of their meeting; which law shall not be passed unless agreed to by a majority of all the members elected to both branches of the General assembly, and which convention, when met, shall have it in their power to revise, amend, or change the constitution.   But, as the holding any part of the human Creation in slavery, or involuntary servitude, can only originate in usurpation and tyranny, no alteration of this constitution shall ever take place so as to introduce slavery or involuntary servitude in this State, otherwise than for the punishment of crimes, whereof the party shall have been duly convicted.

ARTICLE IX.

Sect. 1st.   Knowledge and learning generally diffused, through a community, being essential to the preservation of a free Government, and spreading the opportunities, and advantages of education through the various parts of the Country, being highly conducive to this end, it shall be the duty of the General Assembly to provide, by law, for the improvement of such lands as are, or hereafter may be granted, by the united States to this state, for the use of schools, and to apply any funds which may be raised from such lands, or from any other quarters to the accomplishment of the grand object for which they are or may be intended.   But no lands granted for the use of schools or seminaries of learning shall be sold by authority of this state, prior to the year eighteen hundred and twenty; and the monies which may be raised out of the sale of any such lands, or otherwise obtained for the purposes aforesaid, shall be and remain a fund for the exclusive purpose of promoting the interest of Literature, and the sciences, and for the support of seminaries and public schools. The General Assembly shall from, time to time, pass such laws as shall be calculated to encourage intellectual, Scientifical, and agricultural improvement, by allowing rewards and immunities for the promotion and improvement of arts, sciences, commerce, manufactures, and natural history; and to countenance and encourage the principles of humanity, honesty, industry, and morality.

Sect. 2.   It shall be the duty of the General assembly, as soon as circumstances will permit, to provide, by law, for a general system of education, ascending in a regular gradation, from township schools to a state university, wherein tuition shall be gratis, and equally open to all.

Sect. 3.   And for the promotion of such salutary end, the money which shall be paid, as an equivalent, by persons exempt from militia duty except, in times of war, shall be exclusively, and in equal proportion, applied to the support of County seminaries; also all fines assessed for any breach of the penal laws, shall be applied to said seminaries, in the Counties wherein they shall be assessed.

Sect. 4.   It shall be the duty of the General assembly, as soon as circumstances will permit, to form a penal Code, founded on the principles of reformation, and not of vindictive Justice: and also to provide one or more farms to be an asylum for those persons, who by reason of age, infirmity, or other misfortunes, may have a claim upon the aid and beneficence of society; on such principles, that such persons may therein, find employment, and every reasonable comfort and lose, by their usefulness, the degrading sense of dependence.

Sect. 5.   The General Assembly, at the time they lay off a new County, shall cause, at least, ten per cent to be reserved out of the proceeds of the sale of town lots, in the seat of Justice of such county, for the use of a public library for such County, and at the same session, they shall incorporate a library company, under such rules and regulations as will best secure its permanence, and extend its benefits.

ARTICLE X.

Sect. 1st. There shall not be established or incorporated, in this state, any Bank or Banking company or monied institution, for the purpose of issuing bills of credit, or bills payable to order or bearer; Provided that nothing herein contained shall be so construed as to prevent the General assembly from establishing a State Bank, and branches, not exceeding one branch for any three Counties, and be established at such place, within such Counties, as the directors of the State Bank may select; provided there be subscribed, and paid in specie, on the part of individuals, a sum equal to thirty thousand dollars: Provided also, that the Bank at Vincennes, and the Farmers' and Mechanics' Bank of Indiana, at Madison, shall be considered as incorporated Banks, according to the true tenor of the charters granted to said Banks, by the Legislature of the Indiana Territory: Provided that nothing herein contained shall be so construed, as to prevent the General Assembly from adopting either of the aforesaid Banks as the State Bank: and in case either of them shall be adopted as the State Bank, the other may become a branch, under the rules and regulations herein before prescribed.

ARTICLE XI.

1st. Every person who shall be chosen, or appointed to any office of trust or profit, under the authority of this state, shall, before entering on the duties of said office, take an oath or affirmation, before any person lawfully authorised to administer oaths, to support the constitution of the united States, and the constitution of this state, and also an oath of office.

2d. Treason against this state, shall consist only in levying war against it, in adhering to its enemies, or giving them aid and comfort.

3d. No person shall be convicted of treason, unless on the testimony of two witnesses to the same overt act, or his own confession in open court.

4th. The manner of administering an oath, or affirmation, shall be such as is most consistent with the conscience of the deponent, and shall be esteemed the most solemn appeal to God.

5th.   Every person shall be disqualified from serving as Governor, Lieutenant Governor, Senator, or Representative, for the term for which he shall have been elected, who shall have been convicted of having given, or offered, any bribe, treat, or reward to procure his election.

6th.   All officers shall reside within the state; and all District, County, or Town officers, within their respective Districts, Counties, or towns (the trustees of the town of Clarkesville excepted) and shall keep their respective offices, at such places therein, as may be directed by law; and all Militia officers shall reside within the bounds of the Division, Brigade, Regiment, Battalion or company to which they may severally belong.

7th.   There shall be neither slavery nor involuntary servitude in this state, otherwise than for the punishment of crimes, whereof the party shall have been duly convicted. Nor shall any indenture of any negro or mulatto hereafter made, and executed out of the bounds of this state be of any validity within the state.

8th.   No act of the General assembly shall be in force until it shall have been published in print, unless in cases of emergency.

9th.   All commissions shall be in the name, and by the authority of the State of Indiana; and sealed with the State Seal, and signed by the Governor, and attested by the secretary of state.

10th.   There shall be elected in each county a Recorder, who shall hold his office during the term of seven years, if he shall so long behave well: Provided that nothing herein contained shall prevent the clerks of the circuit Courts from holding the office of recorder.

11th.   Corydon, in Harrison County shall be the seat of Government of the state of Indiana, until the year eighteen hundred and twenty-five, and until removed by law.

12.   The General assembly, when they lay off any new county, shall not reduce the old county, or counties, from which the same shall be taken to a less content than four hundred square miles.

13.   No persons shall hold more than one lucrative office at the same time, except as in this constitution is expressly permitted.

14.   No person shall be appointed as a County officer, within any county, who shall not have been a citizen and an inhabitant

therein one year next preceding his appointment; if the county shall have been so long erected, but if the county shall not have been so long erected, then within the limits of the county or counties, out of which it shall have been taken.

15. All town, and township officers shall be appointed in such manner as shall be directed by law.

16. The following officers of Government shall not be allowed greater annual salaries, until the year eighteen hundred and nineteen than as follows—The Governor one thousand dollars. The Secretary of State, four hundred dollars. The Auditor of public accounts four hundred dollars. the Treasurer four hundred dollars. The Judges of the supreme court eight hundred dollars each. The Presidents of the Circuit Courts eight hundred dollars each, and the members of the General assembly, not exceeding two dollars per day each, during their attendance on the same, and two dollars for every twenty five miles they shall severally travel on the most usual route, in going to, and returning from the General assembly: after which time their pay shall be regulated by law. But no law, passed to increase the pay of the members of the General assembly, shall take effect, until after the close of the session at which such law shall have been passed.

17. In order that the boundaries of the state of Indiana may more certainly be known & established; It is hereby ordained and declared, that the following shall be, and forever remain the boundaries of the said state to wit, Bounded on the east by the meridian line which forms the western boundary of the state of Ohio, On the south by the Ohio river, from the mouth of the Great Miami river, to the mouth of the river Wabash; On the west by a line drawn along the middle of the Wabash river from its mouth to a point, where a due north line drawn from the town of Vincennes, would last touch the northwestern shore of the said Wabash River; and from thence by a due north line until the same shall intersect an east and west line drawn through a point ten miles north of the southern extreme of lake Michigan; On the north by said east and west line, until the same shall intersect the first mentioned meridian line, which forms the western boundary of the State of Ohio.

ARTICLE XII.

Sect. 1st.   That no evils or inconvenience may arise from the change of a Territorial Government to a permanent State Government, it is declared by this Convention that all rights, suits, actions, prosecutions, recognizances, contracts, and claims, both as it respects individuals and bodies corporate, shall continue as if no change had taken place in this Government.

Sect. 2.   All fines penalties and forfeitures, due, and owing to the Territory of Indiana or any County therein, shall inure to the use of the State or County. All bonds executed to the Governor, or any other officer in his official Capacity in the Territory, shall pass over to the Governor or other officers of the State or County, and their successors in office, for the use of the State or County, or by him or them to be respectively assigned over to the use of those concerned as the case may be.

Sect. 3.   The Governor, secretary, and Judges, and all other officers both civil and military, under the Territorial Government, shall continue in the exercise of the duties of their respective departments, until the said officers are superceded under the authority of this constitution.

Sect. 4.   All laws and parts of laws now in force in this Territory not inconsistent with this constitution, shall continue and remain in full force and effect, until they expire or be repealed.

Sect. 5th.   The Governor shall use his private seal, until a state seal be procured.

Sect. 6th.   The Governor, secretary of state, auditor of public accounts, and Treasurer, shall severally reside and keep all the public records books, and papers in any manner relating to their respective offices, at the seat of Government; provided notwithstanding that nothing herein contained shall be so construed, as to affect the residence of the Governor for the space of six months, and until buildings suitable for his accommodation, shall be procured at the expence of the state.

Sect. 7th.   All suits, pleas, plaints and other proceedings now depending in any Court of record or Justices Courts shall be prosecuted to final Judgment and execution and all appeals, writs of error certiorari injunction or other proceedings whatsoever, shall progress and be carried on in the respective Court or Courts in the same manner as is now provided by law, and all proceedings had therein in as full and complete a manner as if this constitution were not adopted. And appeals and writs of error may be taken from the circuit court, and General Court, now established in the Indiana Territory, to the supreme court, in such manner as shall be provided for by law.

Sect. 8.   The President of this convention shall issue writs of election, directed to the several sheriffs of the several Counties, requiring them to cause an election to be held for a Governor, Lieutenant Governor, a Representative to the Congress of the united States, Members of the General Assembly, sheriffs and Coroners, at the respective election districts in each County on the first Monday in August next: which election shall be conducted in the manner prescribed by the existing election laws of the Indiana Territory; and the said Governor, Lieutenant Governor, members of the General Assembly, sheriffs and coroners, then duly elected, shall continue to exercise the duties of their respective offices for the time prescribed by this constitution and until their successor or successors are qualified, and no longer.

Sec. 9.   Until the first enumeration shall be made, as directed by this constitution, the County of Wayne shall be entitled to one senator, and three Representatives; the County of Franklin, one senator, and three Representatives the County of Dearborn, one senator, and two Representatives; the County of Switzerland, one Representative and the County of Jefferson and Switzerland one senator and the County of Jefferson two Representatives; the County of Clark one senator, and three Representatives; the County of Harrison one senator, and three Representatives; the Counties of Washington, Orange, and Jackson one senator and the County of Washington two Representatives; the Counties of Orange and Jackson one Representative each; the County of Knox one senator, and three Representatives; the County of Gibson one senator and two representatives; the Counties of Posey Warrick and Perry one senator, and each of the aforesaid Counties of Posey, Warrick, and Perry, one Representative.

Sect. 10.   All books, records, documents, warrants and papers, appertaining and belonging to the office of the Territorial Treasurer of the Indiana Territory; and all monies therein, and all papers and documents in the office of the Secretary of said Territory, shall be disposed of as the General Assembly of this State may direct.

Sect. 11. All suits, actions, pleas, plaints, prosecutions, and causes whatsoever, and all records, Books, papers and documents now in the General Court, may be transferred to the supreme Court established by this constitution. And all causes, suits, actions, pleas, plaints, and prosecutions whatsoever, now existing or pending in the circuit Courts of this Territory, or which may be therein at the change of Government, and all records, books, papers and documents relating to the said suits, or filed in the said Courts, may be transferred over to the circuit Courts established by this constitution, under such rules and regulations, as the General Assembly may direct.

Done in Convention at Corydon, on the twenty ninth day of June in the year of our Lord eighteen hundred and sixteen, and of the Independence of the United States the fortieth.

In witness whereof we have hereunto subscribed our names.

JONATHAN JENNINGS,
President of the Convention and
Delegate from the County of Clark.

Thomas Carr,
John K. Graham,
James Lemon,
James Scott,

Delegates in Convention from the
County of Clark.

James Dill,
Ezra Ferris,
Solomon Manwaring,

Delegates in Convention from the
County of Dearborn.

James Brownlee,
William H. Eads,
Robert Hanna,
Enoch McCarty,
James Noble,

Delegates in Convention from the
County of Franklin.

Alexander Devin,
Fredc Rapp,   Delegates in Convention from the
David Robb,   County of Gibson.
James Smith,

John Boone,
Davis Floyd,
Daniel C. Lane   Delegates in Convention from the
Dennis Pennington,   County of Harrison.
Patrick Shields,

Nath'l Hunt,
David H. Maxwell,   Delegates in Convention from the
Samuel Smocke,   County of Jefferson.

John Badollet,
John Benefiel,
Jno. Johnson,   Delegates in Convention from the
Wm. Polke,   County of Knox.
B. Parke,

Charles Polke,   Delegate from the County of Perry.
Dann Lynn,   Delegate from the County of Posey.
William Cotton,   Delegate from the County of Switzerland.

John De Pauw,
William Graham,
William Lowe,   [Delegates in Convention from the
Samuel Milroy,   County of Washington.]
Robert McIntire,

Patrick Beard,
Jeremiah Cox,   [Delegates in Convention from the
Hugh Cull,   County of Wayne.]
Joseph Holeman.

Attest,

William Hendricks, Secretary.

RESOLUTION OF ADMISSION, 1816

On December 11, 1816, James Madison, President of the United States, approved the Congressional resolution formally admitting Indiana to the Union. The Road to Statehood was complete and the nineteenth State had a birthday.[34]

Resolution for admitting the State of Indiana into the Union.

Whereas, in pursuance of an act of Congress, passed on the nineteenth day of April, one thousand eight hundred and sixteen, entitled "An act to enable the people of the Indiana Territory to form a constitution and State government, and for the admission of that State into the Union," the people of the said Territory did, on the twenty-ninth day of June, in the present year, by a convention called for that purpose, form for themselves a constitution and State government, which constitution and State government, so formed, is republican, and in conformity with the principles of the articles of compact between the original States and the people and States in the Territory Northwest of the River Ohio, passed on the thirteenth day of July, one thousand seven hundred and eighty-seven:

Resolved by the Senate and House of Representatives of the United States of America in Congress assembled, That the State of Indiana shall be one, and is hereby declared to be one, of the United States of America, and admitted into the Union on an equal footing with the original States, in all respects whatever.

Approved, December 11, 1816.

---

[34] *Annals of Congress,* 14th Cong., 2 Sess., 1348; *U. S. Statutes at Large,* III, 399-400; Kettleborough (ed.), *Constitution Making in Indiana,* I, 129-132.